Bob Geldof

BIOGRAPHY OF BOB

GELDOF

From Band Aid to Live Aid – How One Man's

Determination Fought Hunger and Injustice

Arthur Rush

Bob Geldof

DISCLAIMER

The following book is for entertainment and informational purposes only. The information presented is without contract or any type of guarantee assurance. While every caution has been taken to provide accurate and current information, it is solely the reader's responsibility to check all information contained in this article before relying upon it. Neither the author nor the publisher can be held accountable for any errors or omissions. Under no circumstances will any legal responsibility or blame be held against the author or publisher for any reparation, damages, or monetary loss due to the information presented, either directly or indirectly. This book is not intended as legal or medical advice. If any such specialized advice is needed, seek a qualified individual for help.

Trademarks are used without permission. Use of the trademark is not authorized by, associated with, or sponsored by the trademark owners. All trademarks and brands used within this book are used with no intent to

Bob Geldof

infringe on the trademark owners and are only used for clarifying purposes.

Bob Geldof

TABLE OF CONTENT

Bob Geldof

INTRODUCTION

Bob Geldof's name echoes through the corridors of music, charity, and global activism. He is a man whose life story has captivated millions not because of his fame, but because of his commitment to using that fame for a higher cause. While he is known for his role as the lead singer of the Boomtown Rats, it was his tireless dedication to humanitarian efforts that truly set him apart. Bob Geldof is not just a musician or a philanthropist he is a force for change, one who has used his voice and his platform to bring global attention to issues of inequality, injustice, and suffering. His journey is one that exemplifies the power of action, and it is a story worth telling because it shows what can be accomplished when one person refuses to stand by in the face of injustice.

Bob's life is defined by two parallel tracks: music and activism. His rise to fame came through his music, particularly with the Boomtown Rats, but it wasn't long before he realized that the fame and success he had achieved in the music world could be leveraged for something much greater. When the famine in Ethiopia hit the world's headlines in the early 1980s, Bob could no longer stay silent. He had built a career as a voice for his generation, and now he would use that voice to draw attention to the suffering happening on the other side of the globe. This moment marked the beginning of a new chapter in his life, one where his identity as a musician merged with his identity as a global advocate.

In the years that followed, Bob Geldof would go on to create one of the most monumental charity events in history. Live Aid, a concert aimed at raising funds for the famine-stricken regions of Africa, not only raised millions of dollars, but it also changed the way the world viewed global charity. It wasn't just about giving money, it was about making people care. It was about using music to bring people together from all over the world and demonstrating the transformative power of group action. What started as a simple idea to help those in need became an international movement that demonstrated the power of music to drive social change.

Bob Geldof

This biography takes you behind the scenes of Bob's incredible journey, one that spans not only decades of music history, but also countless humanitarian efforts that have shaped the way we think about global issues. It is a story of triumphs and struggles, of victories and setbacks, but above all, it is a story of a man who never gave up on the world. His commitment to making a difference, whether through his music or his advocacy, has inspired countless individuals to follow in his footsteps. Bob Geldof's life has shown us that one voice, fueled by passion and purpose, can be a catalyst for change.

Through this book, you will discover not just the public Bob Geldof, the man who stood on stage at Wembley and rallied millions, but also the private Bob the father, the husband, the man who has had to navigate the complexities of life, love, and loss while staying true to his mission. In the public eye, Bob has always been larger than life, but behind the scenes, he is just like any other person, struggling with the same emotions, doubts, and fears. The man behind the music and the activism is one of incredible depth and complexity, and this biography will show you the full scope of his journey.

You will encounter Bob's personal battles, including the heartbreak of losing his wife, Paula Yates, and the emotional toll of raising his children as a single father. You will witness his frustration with the system, his relentless drive to bring about change, and his tireless efforts to fight global poverty and inequality. Through his personal and professional life, Bob has always stayed true to one principle: the world can be better, and it's worth fighting for. His story is one of resilience and resolve, of facing the most daunting challenges and continuing to push forward, no matter the obstacles.

Alongside his well-known activism, this biography explores Bob's profound impact on the music industry, his legacy as an artist, and how he transformed the role of the celebrity in global activism. His story is a testament to the belief that fame doesn't have to be just about personal gain, it can be a tool for good. Through his campaigns for debt relief, his commitment to Africa, and his role in raising awareness of issues like climate change and social justice, Bob Geldof has shown that fame can be harnessed to bring about real and lasting change.

As you journey through the pages of this book, you will gain insight into Bob Geldof's mindset and the values that have driven him throughout his life. His philosophy is grounded in the belief that the world should be more just, that people should stand together to fight for equality, and that we all have a role to play in creating a better future. His story is a living example of the power of one person to make a difference, and his legacy is a call to action for all of us.

This biography is not just a story about a rock star who turned into a philanthropist, it's about a man who has spent his life challenging the status quo, fighting for the marginalized, and using his platform to raise awareness about the most pressing global issues of our time. It's an inspiring tale of fervor, tenacity, and an unwavering will to improve the world. Bob Geldof's life shows us that greatness isn't defined by fame or wealth, it's defined by the difference we make in the lives of others.

The following pages will take you on a journey through the life of one of the most influential figures of our time. It's a journey that is both inspiring and humbling, one that reminds us all of the power we have to create change. Bob Geldof's story is far from over, and as you turn these pages, you will understand why his life is one that continues to inspire millions around the world to take action, to care, and to stand up for what is right.

CHAPTER 1: WHO IS BOB GELDOF?

Bob Geldof's name has become synonymous with one of the greatest acts of charity in modern history. A man who, in the blink of an eye, shifted from rock stardom to global humanitarian leadership, Geldof's life is one of remarkable transformation and tireless dedication. But before he became the face of world-changing charity efforts, before the iconic "Live Aid" concerts, and before he raised millions to fight hunger, there was a young man, growing up in Dublin, Ireland, with a sense of urgency and rebellion that would shape his destiny.

Born in the peaceful Dublin suburbs on October 5, 1951, Robert Frederick Zenon Geldof's early years did not foreshadow the spectacular global stage that lay ahead of him. Raised in a modest, working-class family, Bob's world was a far cry from the glamor and excesses of rock and roll. His father, a man who worked as a dairy farmer, was a stern figure, while his mother, a teacher, was nurturing and kind. It was in this home, amidst the contrasting influences of authority and compassion, that Bob first began to feel the stirrings of defiance.

The Geldof household was a place where discipline met love, and it was in this environment that Bob developed his unique mix of charm and aggression. School wasn't a place he particularly enjoyed, though his talent for writing and music began to blossom early. Yet it wasn't academia that called to Bob, it was the beat of rebellion. Dublin in the 1960s was a city brimming with the vibrancy of youth culture, and Bob was drawn to the rising tide of social and political unrest that defined the era. He found his escape in the music of the time, punk rock, which felt like a voice for those who were tired of the status quo.

In his teenage years, the music scene was changing fast, and it wasn't long before Bob found himself at the center of it. After leaving school, he tried his hand at a variety of odd jobs, but it was in music that he truly found himself. By the early 1970s, Bob had joined "The

Boomtown Rats", a band that would soon be catapulted to fame in Ireland and beyond. Formed in 1975, the group became known for their punk-infused rock, with Bob as its frontman and chief songwriter. He was anything but conventional, and his raw energy and cutting-edge lyrics resonated deeply with a generation of young people frustrated by the world around them.

The Boomtown Rats, with their gritty sound and unapologetic style, quickly gained a reputation. Their debut single, "Lookin' After No. 1", hit the charts in 1977, but it was their second single, "Rat Trap", that truly put them on the map. The song was a biting commentary on the limitations of urban life, and its success proved that Bob's voice was more than just a passing trend, it was a force to be reckoned with. The Rats would go on to release several more hits, including "I Don't Like Mondays", a song that became one of the band's most iconic anthems. It was a reflection of Bob's rebellious spirit, and it was clear that he was more than just a musician; he was a commentator on the times, a voice for those who felt unheard.

Bob Geldof

Bob Geldof was defined by more than simply his music, though. There was something more about him, a restless need to make a difference in the world, to not just stand on stage and perform, but to use his influence to change lives. His rise to fame wasn't just about selling records and drawing crowds. It was about using his platform to speak on behalf of those who were suffering. He may have been a rock star, but his eyes were always on the bigger picture. He had seen the injustices in the world, and he wasn't content to just let them pass by. He would be the one to take a stand, no matter the cost.

As the 1980s dawned, Bob's fame continued to grow, but so did his awareness of the world's pressing issues. In particular, he couldn't ignore the images of famine and suffering coming from Africa. The tragic famine in Ethiopia, which began in the early 1980s, hit Bob particularly hard. He had witnessed the stark contrast between his privileged lifestyle and the extreme poverty that millions were facing on a daily basis. It was impossible for him to turn a blind eye.

Still, it wasn't until 1984 that Bob's life would drastically change, turning him from a rock star to a world-renowned humanitarian. That year, Band Aid, the charity supergroup Bob formed, released their iconic single "Do They Know It's Christmas?", and suddenly, Bob was no longer just a musician he was a leader, using his fame and his voice to fight against hunger and injustice. The song was a massive success, but its impact went beyond just raising money. It sparked a revolution of awareness, and it was only the beginning.

The response to Band Aid was overwhelming. Bob was thrust into the spotlight, and with it came an incredible responsibility. It wasn't just about singing a song or performing for the cameras, it was about organizing, motivating, and uniting people to act. He didn't just want to raise money, he wanted to create change, to do something tangible. And so, with characteristic determination, Bob Geldof set his sights on something even more ambitious: the monumental Live Aid concert.

Live Aid, which took place on July 13, 1985, was not just another concert. It was a global event, broadcast to millions of people across the world. For Bob, it was the culmination of years of work, and it would define his legacy. Both in terms of the money raised and the exposure it brought about around the world, Live Aid was a huge success. It showed the power of music to bring people together for a common cause. It was a testament to the fact that one person, no matter their background, could make a difference in the world.

But Bob Geldof was never content to rest on his laurels. Despite the overwhelming success of Live Aid, his work was far from over. He continued to fight for debt relief in Africa, for more effective aid distribution, and for the voices of the marginalized to be heard. He wasn't just a rock star anymore; he had become a global figure, a man who had used his fame to create real, lasting change. His commitment to the cause was unwavering, and it wasn't long before he was back at the forefront of another major campaign, Live 8, in 2005, which sought to bring attention to the issue of world poverty.

Bob Geldof

A rock star and an activist, a critic and a hero, Bob Geldof remained a multifaceted person throughout it all. There were several disagreements along the way. His methods and objectives were questioned by a number of detractors. But for Bob, it was always about the mission. His drive was not rooted in fame or fortune, but in the belief that he could do something to change the world.

Bob Geldof's life is a testament to the power of determination and the impact one individual can have on the world. From his early days in Dublin to his rise to fame with the Boomtown Rats, and ultimately to his transformation into a global humanitarian, Bob has never stopped fighting for what he believes in. He is a man who, through sheer will and vision, turned his music and fame into a platform for change. In doing so, he became an inspiration to millions proving that no matter where you start, with determination, you can change the world.

This is Bob Geldof's story of rock and roll, revolution, and redemption. It's the story of a man who saw the suffering in the world and didn't just look away; he stepped up, used his influence, and made a difference. And while his journey is far from over, one thing is certain: Bob Geldof's legacy will continue to inspire generations to come.

CHAPTER 2: THE CATALYST

It was the early 1980s, and the world was still adjusting to the rapid shifts in politics, music, and media. Bob Geldof, by then already a household name with the Boomtown Rats, had become accustomed to being in the limelight. But fame, as he would soon realize, could be used for something much more profound than just selling records or headlines. Little did he know, a simple broadcast from Ethiopia would ignite the fire in him that would change the course of history.

It all started on a chilly, unremarkable winter evening in 1984. Bob was watching a television program, something that wasn't at the forefront of his mind most of the time. But that night, it was different. The BBC aired a documentary about the famine in Ethiopia. The images were disturbing. Heartbreaking. Thousands of children, their bones visible under thin, gaunt skin, struggling for survival in the face of what seemed like an insurmountable crisis. Bob, like many, was shaken by the scenes. It was difficult to overlook the enormity of the catastrophe and the suffering. The urgency of the situation pressed on him like a weight he couldn't escape.

Bob's mind was in turmoil, but it was also set in motion. He had always believed in using his platform for something greater, but the reality of what was happening in Africa brought everything into sharper focus. It wasn't just a crisis in a far-off country, it was a human crisis. The sense of injustice overwhelmed him, and a question took root in his mind: "What can I do about this?" This wasn't just another charity appeal or vague political message, this was a call to arms. And Bob, with his firebrand personality, wasn't about to turn a blind eye. It wasn't enough to feel sorry for people on the other side of the world. The question had to be answered with action.

In the months following the broadcast, Bob became fixated on the idea of doing something, anything, that could make a difference. His fame and influence, which had once been a means of personal success, suddenly felt like a tool he had to wield for something far more significant. After all, what was fame without purpose? But even with all his celebrity, Bob knew he couldn't do this alone. He would need help; he would need the support of the entire music world to make an impact on such a vast scale. He had the idea: a charity single, sung by some of the biggest names in music, that would raise money for famine relief. But it wasn't just about the money, it was about rallying people, sending a clear message that the world was not indifferent to the suffering. It was time for action. Time for a revolution in how the world viewed charity and the global community.

Geldof wasn't new to the idea of using music for a cause. In fact, music had always been part of his rebellious spirit, his desire to challenge norms and push boundaries. But this would be different. It wasn't about selling records or being in the spotlight. This was about saving lives, making sure the world paid attention, and channeling the energy of popular culture into something meaningful. The idea took shape quickly, and before long, Bob was in full-on planning mode.

The first step was gathering the stars. Bob knew that only a supergroup of musicians would have the pull needed to attract the attention of the media and the masses. He picked up the phone and started calling his peers rock stars, pop icons, and legends who could command a global stage. He had a vision of a group of the biggest names in music, from every genre, coming together for a singular cause. But this was no ordinary collaboration. This was going to be something that had never been done before. He needed musicians who believed in the cause and who were willing to step outside their comfort zones to make a real difference.

The names that Bob managed to bring together were nothing short of remarkable: Bono, Sting, Phil Collins, George Michael, and David Bowie, just to name a few. These were the musicians that the world adored, and Bob knew that their participation would not only bring attention but would also raise unprecedented amounts of money. He didn't just need their voices; he needed their commitment. And they all agreed. They were in. The next hurdle was making the song. Bob had the vision, but he needed the right musical piece to convey the message.

It was clear that the song needed to be both powerful and unforgettable. It had to convey a sense of urgency and also inspire hope. But above all, it had to touch hearts. Bob knew it couldn't be just another charity track. It needed to become a cultural phenomenon, a rallying cry. So, he went to Midge Ure, the frontman of Ultravox, and together they crafted a melody that was both simple and monumental. It had to be something that would be instantly recognizable, something that would stir people to action. And with that, the seeds of Band Aid were sown.

The song that would change everything, "Do They Know It's Christmas?", was born. In just a matter of days, some of the most iconic voices in music converged in a London studio. It was a chaotic and exhilarating experience, with musicians from different genres and backgrounds all coming together for a common cause.

The track was recorded in just one day, a stunning feat given the immense pressure and the short amount of time available. It wasn't about perfection, it was about urgency. The message was clear: the time to act was now.

Released in November 1984, "Do They Know It's Christmas?" became an instant hit. It shot to the top of the charts, selling millions of copies worldwide and raising millions for famine relief. The song was a symbol of collective action, a testament to what could be achieved when musicians and the public came together for a cause greater than themselves. But it wasn't just about the money it was about the awareness it raised. For the first time, the plight of famine-stricken Ethiopia was brought directly into people's homes. It wasn't something happening far away on the evening news, it was something that could no longer be ignored.

The song was a success beyond Bob's wildest expectations. It raised an incredible £8 million for famine relief, but it also set the stage for something even bigger. Bob's vision had never been limited to just a single track. The "Band Aid" song was only the beginning. It had sparked a global conversation, and Bob knew that there was more that could be done. He had stirred the world's conscience, and he wasn't about to stop there. He had begun to realize the full potential of his newfound role not just as a musician but as a global advocate for change.

Despite the success of "Do They Know It's Christmas?" Bob was already planning for the future. He knew the next step was to take this movement to an even grander scale. One song had proven the power of music to raise funds, but now, he wanted to use music to create lasting change. He began planning the next phase of his mission: the Live Aid concerts, which would go on to become the most ambitious and successful live music events ever staged. It was clear to Bob that this was only the beginning. He had started a revolution, a musical revolution that would not only change the world's perception of hunger but also redefine the role of celebrity in the fight against global issues.

And so, in the wake of the Band Aid success, the world's eyes were now on Bob Geldof. What started as a response to a broadcast had grown into something far larger. It wasn't just about hunger anymore it was about using every available tool to bring about change, to show the world that no one was beyond help, and that if people truly cared, they could make a difference. The journey had begun, and Bob was ready for the next chapter. His next act would take him to a new stage, a stage where the world would be watching, waiting to see what this tireless advocate for change would do next.

From a small studio in London to the grandest stages in the world, Bob Geldof's path was set. And it was a path that would forever change the way people viewed the power of music, of celebrity, and of one person's determination to make the world a better place.

CHAPTER 3: THE BAND AID PHENOMENON

It was a cold, bleak winter in 1984 when Bob Geldof's plan began to take shape. The images from Ethiopia's devastating famine were still fresh in his mind. Those haunting scenes had sparked something inside him, a need to do something tangible. The fire had been lit, and now it was time to gather the troops. Bob knew this wouldn't be a solo effort that was going to require the collective might of the music world. If his idea was going to succeed, he needed the best and the brightest, the ones who could move mountains and inspire millions. He needed the stars.

Putting up an all-star group, however, was not going to be simple. Bob was well aware of the egos, the rivalries, and the schedules that would complicate things. After all, he wasn't asking them to perform at the next major concert or show; he was asking for something far more significant: their voices for a cause. There were no guarantees. He had to sell the idea, get people to see the vision, and most importantly, convince them that this wasn't about them, but about something bigger than any of them individually.

Bob's first move was to go straight for the biggest names in the music business, those whose participation would not only raise awareness but would also set a precedent. He made calls to his friends and colleagues, including Sting, Bono, and George Michael. These were the musicians whose influence could not be overstated. They were already global icons, their music had crossed borders, and now, Bob needed their hearts and minds. The conversations were intense but short. They knew the cause was real, and they knew the urgency. Their participation was immediate, but Bob didn't stop there. This wasn't going to be just a handful of famous names. He had a much grander vision.

The next few weeks were a whirlwind of phone calls, meetings, and schedules, as Bob sought out other stars. David Bowie, Phil Collins, and Paul Young all joined the mission. Each one added a layer of credibility and weight to the project. What Bob was assembling wasn't just a band, it was a movement. The stars didn't just offer their voices, they brought their platform, their massive fanbases, and their passion for a cause that transcended anything they had done before.

Bob wasn't just gathering the biggest names in music; he was gathering a group of individuals whose influence reached millions of people around the world. This wasn't going to be a typical charity single. This was a chance to make a statement, a way to use the power of celebrity to change the way the world viewed famine and aid. Bob was thinking bigger than just a song; he was thinking about the global implications of what they could achieve together.

Despite the stellar lineup of musicians, there was still a lot of work to be done. Band Aid had to come together quickly, and there was little time for the sort of polished, pre-planned event that would usually take months. This wasn't a tour or a concert that could be mapped out over time. This was a one-off recording session that would have to be completed in a matter of days. The urgency of the situation was clear to everyone involved. They needed to move fast.

It wasn't just about picking up the phone and getting people to show up. Bob had to make sure the song's message was clear, that the lyrics were precise and evocative. The track had to be a direct call to action. Bob worked with Midge Ure, the frontman of Ultravox, to craft the perfect anthem, something that was easy to understand but hard to forget. It needed to capture both the pain of the suffering and the hope for change. They wanted people to not just donate money but to feel an emotional connection to the cause. Bob and Midge went to work, and within a matter of days, "Do They Know It's Christmas?" was born.

The recording of the song itself was an intense, chaotic experience. Bob had orchestrated this session with the precision of a conductor. The pressure was immense. There was no time to waste, no room for error. It was a testament to Bob's relentless drive that he kept everyone focused on the task at hand. The stars who gathered in the studio had no illusions about the magnitude of what they were doing. This wasn't just a music project, it was history in the making.

The atmosphere in the studio was electric. Musicians who were usually seen on stage with their own bands, in their own worlds, came together to sing a song with a singular purpose. It was surreal to see these legends, who had spent years making music for millions, now singing for something far more significant than any chart-topping hit. Each one of them brought their own unique style to the track, and Bob, ever the perfectionist, made sure that every voice was given its moment.

Bob was everywhere directing, encouraging, and occasionally making sure the right notes were hit. He wasn't just a rock star now; he was the project manager of something much bigger than himself. He worked tirelessly to keep the energy up, to remind everyone why they were there. It was clear to them all that this wasn't a usual recording session. This was something that could change the world.

Once the song was recorded, the hard work didn't stop. Bob and his team worked around the clock to get it ready for release. It wasn't just about getting the song onto the radio it was about creating a cultural event, something that would spark a movement. The single had to be released fast, and the marketing campaign was just as crucial as the song itself. Bob was determined to make sure the song reached every corner of the globe, and he succeeded. The track hit the airwaves with the force of a freight train.

Upon its release, "Do They Know It's Christmas?" was an instant success. It skyrocketed to the top of the charts in the UK, and its impact was felt far beyond the world of music. It wasn't just about the money raised (although that was significant). The song's success was a wake-up call to millions around the world. The famine in Ethiopia was no longer a distant tragedy that people read about in the newspaper. It was a cause that millions of people, through the power of music, could now rally behind.

But Bob wasn't content to sit back and bask in the success. The song's commercial success was merely a reflection of its deeper impact. "Do They Know It's Christmas?" wasn't just a hit it was a catalyst for change. Bob's vision was becoming a reality, but there was more to do. He was already thinking ahead to the next step, the next level of impact. The money raised was just the beginning. Bob knew that the cause needed something far more ambitious.

By the end of 1984, "Do They Know It's Christmas?" had raised millions of dollars, but it also laid the groundwork for what would become one of the most iconic and impactful charity events in history, Live Aid. The success of Band Aid had shown Bob what was possible when people came together for a common cause. It had proven that music could unite people on a massive scale, and Bob knew that if he could harness that power again, it could create a seismic shift in the way the world approached global crises.

In many ways, the Band Aid phenomenon was a masterclass in leveraging celebrity and media for good. It showed that no matter how big or small, anyone could contribute to the fight against global injustice. Bob's tireless work in organizing the single and ensuring it reached as many people as possible set the stage for even bigger campaigns. What had started as an idea sparked by a television broadcast had now grown into a worldwide movement. And Bob, ever determined, wasn't stopping until the fight was won.

In the months that followed, Bob was inundated with praise, but he didn't let it distract him. His focus remained fixed on the cause. The millions raised by Band Aid were only the beginning. There was still so much to be done. And with the world's attention now firmly on Ethiopia, Bob knew the next step was going to be the biggest challenge of his career Live Aid. This was just the beginning of a movement that would go on to raise millions more and solidify Bob Geldof's place in history as one of the most influential figures of his generation.

As Bob looked back on the success of Band Aid, he couldn't help but feel a sense of pride. He had done it. He had gathered the stars, created a song that resonated with people around the world, and raised millions of pounds for famine relief. The movement was born, but Bob wasn't resting. The next challenge loomed large, and he was more determined than ever to keep pushing forward. "Do They Know It's Christmas?" had ignited something in Bob, and he wasn't going to let it fizzle out. The world was watching, and Bob Geldof was ready to answer the call.

Bob Geldof

CHAPTER 4: THE LIVE AID VISION

In the wake of Band Aid's unexpected success, Bob Geldof's vision shifted into overdrive. He had achieved something many believed impossible: a single song had raised millions of dollars and shone a glaring light on the humanitarian crisis in Ethiopia. Yet, Bob knew this was only the beginning. The weight of the world's attention now rested on his shoulders, and he realized that if he truly wanted to change the way people viewed global poverty and injustice, he had to go even further. The idea of Live Aid began to take form in his mind not as a mere concert, but as a seismic event, a symbol of the world coming together to fight famine and oppression.

The magnitude of the idea didn't hit Bob immediately. It wasn't like snapping his fingers and having everything fall into place. This would require the kind of energy and dedication that only someone like him, with a deep sense of purpose and urgency, could muster. The vision was clear: a global concert, a musical spectacle unlike any other, where the world's most famous artists would perform live, all for a single cause. It wasn't enough to just raise money anymore; he wanted to shift the very cultural landscape. Bob envisioned Live Aid as not only a fundraiser but also a statement. It would be an event that would live on in history, an example of what could happen when the music world came together with a common purpose.

From the start, Bob knew that for Live Aid to be truly global, it needed a grand, expansive vision. The idea of a single concert was far too small. This had to be bigger. Bob's brain worked quickly, mapping out how to pull this off. The world had never seen anything like it before. He had already proved that music could bring people together for a cause with "Do They Know It's Christmas?"; now, he had to make this dream even bigger. A global concert that would be broadcast simultaneously across the world seemed like an audacious idea, but Bob was never one to shy away from the impossible. The scale of the vision made him realize that he would need an army of people, organizers, technicians, media outlets, and, of course, the artists themselves.

Bob started reaching out to key figures in the music world, and this time, it wasn't just about asking for a song or a performance. He was asking for their commitment to something that could potentially change the course of history. He needed people who didn't just want to show up for a quick charity event. He needed people who would commit themselves to the cause, people who understood the weight of what they were being asked to do. Bob knew that the right artists could make this event resonate with millions, and he started pulling together an extraordinary lineup.

Some of the biggest names in music immediately jumped at the chance to be part of Live Aid. Bowie. The Rolling Stones. U2. Queen. Each of these artists had the kind of reach that could make the event global in the truest sense. But Bob didn't stop there. He needed the perfect mix of rock legends, pop stars, and even a few surprise acts who would create the magic and energy required to keep the audience hooked. It wasn't just about filling the stage, it was about telling the story of the world through music. And when you gather the best, you have a chance to create something unforgettable.

It wasn't just about the music. Bob had to work tirelessly with the logistics team to make sure that the event could live up to its grand ambitions. He wasn't just orchestrating a concert; he was orchestrating a movement. The technical side of Live Aid would need to be flawless. This was a concert that would span continents, with performances coming from multiple cities, from London to Philadelphia, and later other major locations. The logistics were dizzying. Everything had to be carefully planned and executed to ensure smooth transitions, no hiccups, no downtime, just pure, uninterrupted music for the cause.

The two major locations were Wembley Stadium in London and JFK Stadium in Philadelphia. Each would be home to a variety of international acts, ensuring that the event had global reach. To pull this off, Bob would need media partners who could broadcast the event to millions of viewers around the world. Without them, the scale of Live Aid would be nowhere near what he envisioned. Bob was no stranger to the media, but this was an entirely new beast. He was pushing for live satellite feeds, cutting-edge technology, and creative partnerships to ensure that the message reached every corner of the globe. This wasn't just a rock concert, it was a full-blown media event, broadcasting the urgency of the crisis and turning the plight of Ethiopia into a global conversation.

Planning the performances was another monumental task. Bob needed the artists to understand the weight of what they were doing. This wasn't just a typical gig. Every performance would be a message and an emotional plea for change. The artists had to be ready to give their all, and they had to understand that their participation was about more than just their own spotlight. It was about making sure that every note played, every lyric sung, was in service of something far greater than the music itself. Bob worked closely with the performers, rehearsing the songs that would become anthems of the day. The rehearsal sessions were grueling but filled with energy and enthusiasm. There was no room for egos, only the shared desire to make a difference.

When the day of Live Aid arrived, the world was watching. Bob had carefully crafted this global spectacle, but he also understood the power of the media to bring people into the fold. He knew that millions would be tuning in, their eyes fixed on the live broadcasts, and he was determined that no one would leave the event untouched. The artists performed with the kind of passion that only a cause like this could inspire. There was no distinction between the rockers and pop stars; everyone, from Phil Collins to Madonna, was there to do their part for a world in need.

The moment Queen took the stage, it became clear that this event was transcending entertainment. Freddie Mercury's performance was nothing short of legendary.

With his charismatic presence, he captured the hearts of millions, uniting a divided audience with the sheer force of his performance. It wasn't just about hitting the high notes; it was about creating an atmosphere where every person in that stadium, and every person watching on TV, felt connected to the cause. Queen's set, in particular, became one of the defining moments of the day. It wasn't just a performance, it was a manifestation of what Live Aid stood for: unity, passion, and the power of music to bring about change.

Back in Philadelphia, the energy was just as high. The stadium was packed, and the American audience was just as engaged. One of the most powerful aspects of Live Aid was that it wasn't just about raising money; it was about raising awareness. The broadcast of the event brought the issue of famine to living rooms across the globe. People were no longer able to dismiss the issue as something happening far away. It was right in front of them, in their homes, their televisions, their radios. The media blitz that Bob and his team had worked so hard to secure was paying off, and the results were impossible to ignore. The world was listening.

For Bob, the success of Live Aid wasn't just in the millions of dollars raised, it was in the collective action and the palpable shift in global consciousness. The event showed that a few individuals, bound together by a common cause, could make an immense difference. As the hours passed and the music blared across continents, Bob saw the realization of his vision: a world united in the face of suffering. The collective power of music, when harnessed for a cause, had the potential to do more than entertain it could save lives.

As the last notes of the final song echoed through the stadiums, Bob's heart swelled with a sense of accomplishment. The crowds were chanting, the world was buzzing, and the world's media was covering the event like nothing before it. Live Aid had lived up to its promise, and then some. It wasn't just a concert, it had been a global movement, a call to action that reverberated around the world.

Bob, standing in the background of the spectacle, watched it all unfold. This wasn't just about him. It wasn't about the artists or the celebrities or even the concert itself. It was about something far greater. Bob had succeeded in turning his vision into reality, and now the world would never look at global hunger in the same way again.

The success of Live Aid marked a turning point. For Bob, it was validation of everything he had believed in the power of music, the power of people coming together, and the ability of a single voice to lead a movement. And though the work was far from over, Live Aid had set a new standard for what it meant to fight for change. The world had seen what was possible when passion, talent, and determination were harnessed for a common cause. And for Bob Geldof, this was only the beginning of a lifelong commitment to fighting for those who had no voice.

CHAPTER 5: THE DAY THAT CHANGED THE WORLD

July 13, 1985, is a date that has been etched into the history of music, charity, and global activism. That day, the world came together like never before, united by one cause: to end hunger and bring awareness to the devastating famine in Ethiopia. It wasn't just another day on the calendar, it was the day that Bob Geldof's vision for Live Aid came to life, and with it, the world saw what could be accomplished when people put aside their differences and worked together for something greater.

For months, Bob and his team had worked tirelessly behind the scenes to turn this grand idea into reality. The pressure was immense, but so was the resolve. Bob knew that this event had to be perfect, that every detail had to come together seamlessly. Every moment, every performance, every word spoken would be scrutinized by millions. But the stakes were too high to back down. There was no time for second-guessing. The people who had committed to this cause, the artists, the volunteers, and the media partners, were all ready. They were about to make history.

As the sun rose on that historic day, the sense of anticipation in the air was palpable. The world was waiting for Live Aid to begin. People from all walks of life had gathered in front of their televisions, radios, and even at venues to be part of this groundbreaking event. It wasn't just a concert; it was a collective movement that had the power to change the world. People who had never given much thought to global poverty or famine now found themselves emotionally invested in the cause, united by music and the desire to make a difference.

The two main venues for Live Aid were Wembley Stadium in London and JFK Stadium in Philadelphia, and both were filled to capacity. The significance of these two venues wasn't lost on anyone. These were iconic locations, chosen for their ability to accommodate massive audiences and for their central role in shaping music history. Wembley, the birthplace of legendary concerts, and JFK Stadium, where the energy of rock and roll had sparked cultural revolutions, would now serve as the backdrop for an even greater moment in time.

The clock struck noon in London, and the world held its breath. The first chords of the Live Aid concert reverberated through the massive Wembley Stadium. The crowd went wild, their energy palpable. It was as if the collective heartbeat of the world was beating in time with the music. Bob, though busy behind the scenes, couldn't help but feel a surge of emotion as the first notes of "Bohemian Rhapsody" played across the stadium. Queen's iconic performance was about to begin, and the magic that would unfold in the next few hours was about to change everything.

The crowd at Wembley roared with excitement as Freddie Mercury, the incomparable frontman of Queen, took the stage. His presence was magnetic. There was no mistaking it this was a performance for the ages. Freddie didn't just sing; he commanded the stage with a passion that transcended music itself. He understood the magnitude of what was happening, and he gave it everything he had. The energy was electric. The audience in Wembley Stadium responded with a deafening cheer, their collective enthusiasm filling the stadium and spilling out across the globe through the live broadcast.

Freddie's voice soared as he and Queen belted out "Radio Ga Ga", "We Are the Champions", and, of course, "Bohemian Rhapsody". The whole world watched in awe as one of the greatest rock performances ever unfolded before them. It wasn't just about the songs, it was about what they represented. Queen had managed to transcend the boundaries of the concert stage. They had become part of something far greater than entertainment. They were speaking to the hearts of millions, making history with every note.

At the same time, over 3,000 miles away in Philadelphia, JFK Stadium was coming alive with energy. The American crowd had been just as eager for the event, knowing that the stakes were just as high on their side of the Atlantic. The performances in Philadelphia were just as electric. U2, a band that was quickly becoming one of the most powerful forces in rock, took the stage. Bono's voice was raw with emotion as he led the band through "Bad". The crowd responded in kind, their energy an outpouring of support for a cause that transcended national boundaries.

What made Live Aid truly unique was the sheer scale of the event. It wasn't just about the musical performances, it was about the awareness it brought to the people watching. In homes across the globe, people saw their favorite musicians not just performing, but fighting for change. The concerts were broadcast live via satellite, making it a truly global event. For the first time in history, people from all corners of the earth were tuned in to one singular cause. It wasn't just about watching a concert, it was about being part of something much bigger.

In London, the performances kept coming. David Bowie took to the stage with his usual charisma and flair. His performance of "Heroes" became a defining moment of Live Aid, and the crowd in Wembley swelled with pride, the power of music washing over them. Every performance was met with thunderous applause. Each act knew the weight of what they were doing. They weren't just playing for their fans they were playing for a cause that would be remembered for generations.

The artists gave everything they had. Phil Collins played in both Wembley and JFK Stadium, flying across the Atlantic in a helicopter to make sure his performances were heard in both places. His commitment was an embodiment of the spirit of Live Aid unified, relentless, and passionate.

But beyond the performances, what truly set Live Aid apart was the unprecedented generosity of the viewers. People around the world began making donations, understanding that their contributions were making a tangible difference. The phone lines lit up as donations poured in, with the number climbing higher and higher. It wasn't just about the music, it was about the real, lasting impact that the funds raised could have on the people suffering from famine in Ethiopia and other parts of Africa.

The numbers were staggering. By the end of the day, the total amount raised for famine relief had reached over £150 million. It was an amount that far surpassed anyone's expectations. Bob, who had spearheaded the effort, was elated but never one to bask in the glory. For him, the success of Live Aid wasn't about the money it was about the awareness it brought and the global unity it achieved. The outpouring of support showed the world what could be accomplished when people from all walks of life came together for a common cause.

The world was watching, and for one brief, extraordinary day, it felt as if the entire planet was united. People from different countries, cultures, and backgrounds stood side by side, all connected by the simple, undeniable truth: we are all in this together. Live Aid wasn't just a concert; it was a celebration of humanity's capacity to care, to act, and to change the world.

When the final notes of the last performance echoed through the speakers, and the last donations had been tallied, the world knew that Live Aid had been more than just a one-day event. It was a moment of profound unity, a moment where the power of music transcended borders and politics, bringing people together for something greater than themselves. It wasn't just the artists who had given; it was the people watching, the millions who had made the commitment to help, who had changed the world that day.

The success of Live Aid marked a turning point in global activism. Bob Geldof had proven that music could do more than entertain, it could change the world. Live Aid had set a precedent for how artists, entertainers, and the public could come together to tackle some of the world's most pressing issues. The concert had created a blueprint for future efforts, showing that the world of entertainment could be a powerful force for social change.

As the world moved forward from that unforgettable day, the impact of Live Aid lingered. It wasn't just the money that had been raised, it was the awareness, the partnerships, and the momentum that carried forward. For Bob Geldof, it wasn't about resting on his laurels; the fight was far from over. Live Aid had changed the world, but the work was just beginning.

That day, July 13, 1985, had set the world on fire. It had ignited a spark that would continue to burn brightly for years to come. And as Bob Geldof looked back at what had been accomplished, he knew that the greatest achievement was not the amount of money raised or the star-studded performances, it was the realization that when people come together, they can achieve the impossible. Live Aid had proven that to the world, and for that, it would remain a defining moment in history forever.

CHAPTER 6: THE AFTERMATH

The world had just witnessed something that seemed almost impossible, an event that brought people together across the globe, united by a single cause. Live Aid had set a precedent for what could be achieved when music, celebrity, and collective action came together for something far greater than entertainment. The world had watched as the greatest artists of the era performed not just for applause, but for a cause that transcended borders, ideologies, and nations. As the last notes of the performances faded and the lights dimmed, the question remained: What would come next? What was the lasting impact of Live Aid, and how would the funds raised and the awareness sparked shape the future?

The numbers were staggering, a true testament to the power of people coming together for a cause. The funds raised from Live Aid reached a breathtaking \$125 million. This wasn't just a sum, it was a lifeline for millions of people in Ethiopia and beyond. In an era where the most significant charitable contributions often came from large organizations and governments, Live Aid had demonstrated that individual action, sparked by the energy of a single event, could match or even surpass what governments were able or willing to do. Bob Geldof had proven that a concert could be more than just an entertainment spectacle. It could be a force for real change.

The money raised was a huge accomplishment, but it wasn't the end of the story. Raising money was one thing, distributing it effectively and ensuring it made a tangible difference was an entirely different challenge. This was where the true test of the event's legacy would lie. In the aftermath of Live Aid, Bob and his team had to navigate the complexities of aid distribution. It wasn't enough to just raise the money and hope for the best; they had to ensure that the funds were used effectively, reaching those who needed it most, and that the relief was being delivered in a way that would make a long-term impact.

This was no small task. Aid distribution is a delicate process that requires careful planning, coordination, and transparency. The money had been raised with the best of intentions, but turning that funding into real-world change meant working with the right organizations, cutting through red tape, and ensuring that the aid wasn't just a temporary solution but part of a sustainable effort to address the root causes of poverty and famine. In the months that followed, Bob Geldof and his team worked tirelessly with organizations on the ground in Ethiopia and other affected areas to ensure that the funds were used in a meaningful way.

The formation of the Band Aid Trust, which was established to supervise the distribution of the money received from the Live Aid performances, was one of the most significant elements of this endeavor. The Trust became a central part of the aftermath of Live Aid, ensuring that the money was channeled into projects that had a lasting impact on communities. It wasn't just about sending food and medical supplies, it was about creating long-term infrastructure and supporting projects that could help build a better future for those affected by famine. The Trust worked closely with international organizations, NGOs, and local governments to ensure the funds were being used where they were needed most.

While the money raised was undoubtedly critical, the awareness that Live Aid generated was perhaps the most lasting legacy of the event. Before Live Aid, the famine in Ethiopia had been a tragedy that many people had heard about, but it was still a distant issue for most. People knew about the suffering, but it wasn't something that seemed personal to them. However, when Bob Geldof and the artists of Band Aid stepped into the global spotlight, they changed that dynamic. Live Aid brought the crisis to the forefront of global consciousness in a way that had never been done before.

Television broadcasts, radio stations, and newspapers carried the stories of the famine, the images of the starving children, and the pleas for help, but it was Live Aid that made the world stop and listen. It wasn't just about raising money it was about creating a cultural shift. People could no longer ignore the suffering. The event had made the crisis personal for millions of people across the world. It was no longer something happening "over there" ; it was something that required action from everyone. The artists who performed, the people who donated, and the millions who watched from their living rooms were now connected to the crisis in a way that couldn't be undone.

This global awareness had a profound effect on the way people viewed poverty, hunger, and international aid. It wasn't just about giving money; it was about creating a sense of shared responsibility. The events of Live Aid marked the beginning of a new era in philanthropy, one where people understood that they had the power to make a difference and that the world's problems could no longer be ignored. Bob Geldof's vision had shifted the conversation, making it clear that global issues like hunger were not just a matter of charity, but of global solidarity. Live Aid had united millions of people around the world who otherwise might never have been aware of the scale of the suffering. It had raised a sense of collective responsibility that would inspire countless future efforts to fight hunger, injustice, and poverty.

The impact of Live Aid went far beyond the day of the concerts. In the years that followed, the event set the stage for other global charity initiatives, influencing the way artists, entertainers, and the public engaged with global issues. The idea of using music to raise awareness and drive change became a model for future charitable events. Live Aid proved that entertainment wasn't just for entertainment's sake it could be a powerful vehicle for change. It also set a precedent for how stars could leverage their platforms for the greater good. Celebrities and artists, many of whom had been seen as self-serving or disconnected from the real-world problems that plagued the poor, were now viewed as key figures in the fight for justice.

The event's lasting legacy went beyond raising money for Ethiopia. It changed the way people thought about charity. It moved the conversation away from the typical charity model, which often involved sending a check and hoping for the best, and instead brought people into the process, making them active participants in the fight against poverty. It was a shift from passive giving to active involvement, from simply donating to taking an active stand on global issues. The spirit of Live Aid encouraged people to think about how they could contribute in their own way, how they could use their voice, their resources, or their talent to help solve the world's most pressing problems.

In the years that followed, Bob Geldof's activism didn't slow down. He continued to use his platform to speak out about global issues. His work didn't end with Live Aid or Band Aid; it expanded into new initiatives aimed at tackling the root causes of poverty and injustice. In the years after Live Aid, Bob was involved in numerous campaigns for debt relief in Africa, advocating for policies that would allow impoverished nations to break free from the cycle of debt that had kept them impoverished for so long.

For Bob, the aftershocks of Live Aid weren't about basking in the glory of what had been accomplished. They were about pushing for more. Live Aid had proven that it was possible to bring the world's attention to an issue, to rally people behind a cause, and to raise unprecedented sums of money. Now, the question was: How could that momentum be used to create lasting change? Bob knew that the fight was far from over. The millions of dollars raised were just the beginning, and the awareness generated by the event needed to be channeled into sustained efforts.

As he reflected on the aftermath of Live Aid, Bob saw it as a turning point, a moment when the world realized its collective power. For the first time, millions of people had come together for a cause that went beyond borders and politics. The legacy of Live Aid wasn't just about the funds raised or the artists who performed; it was about the moment when the world realized that change was possible, that a few individuals could make a difference, and that together, humanity could fight back against hunger, injustice, and suffering.

Bob had succeeded in proving that music, celebrity, and global activism could make a real, lasting difference. And as he continued his work in the years that followed, Live Aid remained a shining example of what could be achieved when people were willing to step outside their comfort zones and unite for a common cause. The legacy of that historic day, July 13, 1985, was far-reaching. It changed how the world viewed charity, how it approached global crises, and how it understood its collective responsibility to help those in need. The effects of Live Aid rippled through history, and Bob Geldof had become an indelible figure in the fight for a better world.

CHAPTER 7: THE CRITICISMS

Live Aid had been an overwhelming success, the kind of event that most would call a triumph. It had brought millions together, raised unprecedented amounts of money, and raised awareness for a crisis that had previously been ignored by much of the world. It showed the power of music, celebrity, and collective action to move mountains. But as with any groundbreaking effort, there were those who weren't so quick to offer their praise. For all the accolades and admiration that Bob Geldof received, there were just as many critics, some of whom would cast a long shadow over his legacy. The scrutiny that followed Live Aid didn't come from a few isolated voices; it came from multiple directions, and it forced Bob to confront uncomfortable questions about the true impact of his work.

For the media, Bob Geldof was both a hero and a target. While the press lauded his determination, drive, and success in raising millions, they were also quick to find flaws. Some felt that Bob, in his role as the public face of the event, had taken too much credit for something that was ultimately a collaborative effort. Others felt that his role in orchestrating the event had been more about his own fame and personal legacy than about the cause itself. The British media, in particular, scrutinized him, questioning his motives and even the long-term effectiveness of the funds raised.

The most consistent and prominent criticism leveled at Bob Geldof after Live Aid was what many perceived as a lack of transparency in the distribution of the funds. Some aid organizations and critics believed that, despite the enormous sums of money raised, the funds didn't reach those in need as efficiently or effectively as they could have. They accused Bob and the Band Aid Trust of not properly overseeing how the money was being allocated, and of not ensuring that the funds were used in a sustainable way. The success of the event had highlighted the widespread attention being paid to famine relief, but some believed that the follow-through left much to be desired.

Aid mismanagement became one of the key talking points for those who sought to undermine the credibility of Live Aid. They questioned whether the money was being spent in the right places. Some even suggested that the sheer volume of funds raised had created a bureaucratic mess that hindered progress, with various organizations and governments fighting for control over how the aid should be distributed. Critics argued that, with so many parties involved, the original mission of Live Aid helping the people of Ethiopia had been diluted by inefficiency and poor organization.

Bob Geldof, who had worked tirelessly to raise the funds, found himself facing the heat for decisions that were often beyond his control. He had no illusion about the complexity of aid distribution, but the growing chorus of complaints left him defensive. He had expected criticism that came with the territory of being a public figure, especially one who had orchestrated such a large-scale event. What Bob hadn't anticipated was how deeply the criticisms would affect him and the cause he had so fervently championed. He was thrust into the uncomfortable position of defending his integrity and the methods of distribution against an increasingly vocal opposition.

At the heart of these criticisms was the underlying concern that Live Aid had become too focused on the spectacle of the event itself and not enough on the long-term solutions for Ethiopia and other areas affected by famine. While the money raised had been massive, many felt that the public focus on the concert had overshadowed the real work that needed to be done on the ground. Some of the critics argued that, in creating a media spectacle, Live Aid may have contributed more to celebrity culture than to sustainable aid efforts. To them, the money raised was just a drop in the bucket compared to the long-term investments required to address the root causes of famine and poverty.

The criticisms didn't stop at aid distribution. There was also a cultural sensitivity issue. For all of Bob's passion and drive to make a difference, there were questions about whether his approach was truly sensitive to the cultures and communities that were being helped. Some suggested that the Western-centric view of "saving" Ethiopia wasn't as empowering as it appeared. Were they truly helping the people, or were they imposing their own solutions on communities without consulting them first? These questions, though uncomfortable for Bob, were valid concerns raised by those who saw Live Aid as not just a charity event, but a form of cultural intervention that ignored the autonomy of the very people it sought to help.

Bob had always been a man of action, not of words. He had poured his heart and soul into Live Aid, and his commitment to the cause was undeniable. But now, as the criticisms mounted, he was faced with the task of defending his decisions publicly. The media scrutiny was unrelenting, and Bob was often asked whether he truly understood the complex dynamics at play. Was he, as some critics suggested, a well-intentioned celebrity who had jumped into the deep end without fully understanding the consequences? Or was he a leader with a vision that was always focused on one thing: making a difference?

Bob's response to these criticisms was blunt and unapologetic. He didn't shy away from the tough questions, but he also didn't let anyone undermine his intentions. His position was simple: he had acted with the best of intentions, using every tool at his disposal to bring global attention to the famine. He argued that if he hadn't done what he did, if he hadn't used his celebrity status and musical connections to pull off Live Aid, the crisis in Ethiopia would have remained just that a distant tragedy, far removed from the everyday lives of those living in the West. The sheer scale of Live Aid, in his eyes, was the message it was about waking up the world to the suffering, not just writing a check.

On the issue of aid mismanagement, Bob was forthright. He acknowledged the difficulties inherent in such a large-scale operation, but he didn't believe that this detracted from the overall impact of the event. He argued that while there were certainly logistical challenges, they should not overshadow the success of Live Aid in mobilizing global efforts to address hunger. In his view, no amount of criticism would diminish the fact that Live Aid had, for the first time, shown the world that hunger wasn't just a distant problem, it was everyone's problem.

On the cultural sensitivity issue, Bob was just as resolute. He rejected the notion that his efforts were born out of a colonial mentality or a belief in Western superiority. For him, the idea that the people of Ethiopia or other famine-stricken nations needed to be "saved" by the West was absurd. He didn't see Live Aid as a charity driven by a savior complex, but as a call for global solidarity. His argument was that no one should be ashamed to offer help when it was needed. If the people of Ethiopia were to have a voice, it had to be through the actions of those who were in a position to act. Bob saw Live Aid not as an imposition, but as an opportunity to give those suffering a chance at survival. It wasn't about making the West feel good, it was about offering real solutions to a real problem.

As the criticisms continued to pour in, Bob's determination didn't waver. His stance was clear: he wasn't going to apologize for the success of Live Aid. He had used his fame and influence to spark a global conversation about hunger, and no one could take that away from him. The criticisms, however valid they may have been, were not going to overshadow the undeniable fact that Live Aid had changed the world's approach to philanthropy, activism, and the role of entertainment in social change. Bob had turned his vision into reality, and for that, he would always be proud.

Through all the media scrutiny, the accusations, and the doubts cast on his methods, Bob Geldof remained one of the world's most passionate and vocal advocates for change. He understood that no great movement was without its challenges, and he was willing to face those challenges head-on. The critics were always going to be there, but they couldn't take away what had been accomplished. Live Aid wasn't just an event, it was a watershed moment in history, and Bob Geldof was the man who had made it all possible. The criticisms may have stung, but they didn't change the fact that millions of lives had been saved and the world had been forced to pay attention.

CHAPTER 8: BEYOND MUSIC

Bob Geldof's impact went far beyond the music world. In the wake of his success with Band Aid and Live Aid, he found himself standing at a crossroads; he had ignited the world's conscience with his music, but the next step was not to bask in the glory of past achievements. Bob was a man driven by urgency, by the constant pressure to do more, to be more. Music had been his gateway to global awareness, but now he was thinking bigger. He understood that systemic change couldn't come from a few benefit concerts alone. If he wanted to make lasting change, he needed to get into the heart of the problem. And the problem, in his eyes, was the overwhelming debt that many African nations were burdened with, which was preventing these countries from growing, from investing in the future, and from lifting themselves out of poverty.

Bob Geldof

In the years following Live Aid, Bob's focus shifted toward political advocacy. He became increasingly vocal about the need to reform the way the global economic system treated developing nations, particularly those in Africa. The issues of debt relief and international trade were central to his thinking. Bob understood that charity alone wouldn't solve the deeper, systemic issues. Giving food and aid was vital in the short term, but for long-term change to occur, there needed to be a radical shift in the way the world's wealthiest countries engaged with the poorest nations.

At the heart of Bob's political advocacy was the belief that the West had a responsibility to help create the conditions necessary for African countries to thrive independently. He saw the imposition of crushing debt loads on countries that were already struggling to meet their basic needs as not just an economic issue, but a moral one. The billions of dollars in debt that many African nations owed to Western countries and international institutions were not loans in the traditional sense; they were a form of economic bondage. And Bob was determined to change that. His approach was not subtle. He spoke with the same intensity, urgency, and force that had made him famous as a musician. He wasn't just asking for debt relief, he was demanding it. He wanted to challenge the status quo, to push for the kind of systemic change that would allow African nations to stand on their own feet, without the shackles of debt preventing their progress.

His advocacy for debt relief became one of the most defining elements of his post-Live Aid career. In the late 1990s, Bob began working with other activists and world leaders to create a global movement for debt forgiveness. He wasn't alone in this effort, but his influence was undeniable. He used his high-profile status to bring attention to the issue, speaking at international summits and using the media to amplify his message. Bob didn't just make speeches or write articles he got his hands dirty. He lobbied governments, worked with international organizations, and took every opportunity to hammer home the message that debt relief was not just a good idea, it was an imperative.

The efforts to secure debt relief were not without resistance. The global financial institutions that had been part of the system for decades, institutions like the International Monetary Fund (IMF) and the World Bank, were not eager to forgive debt. They argued that forgiving the debts of developing nations would undermine the stability of the global financial system. But Bob wasn't one to back down. He argued that the system itself was broken. He pointed out that the terms of the loans that African nations had been forced to accept were often exploitative, with interest rates that kept countries in perpetual poverty. It wasn't just a financial issue; it was a human rights issue. Bob's relentless advocacy for debt relief garnered significant attention, and over time, the pressure mounted on governments and financial institutions to take action.

Bob's influence didn't stop with his advocacy for debt relief. He also understood that the world's political leaders had a responsibility to address the underlying causes of poverty. He began to work more closely with world leaders, not just as an activist, but as a strategic ally in the fight against global poverty. His blunt style and directness made him a powerful voice in political circles, and his ability to navigate the complexities of international diplomacy made him an effective advocate for change. Bob was no longer just the frontman of a rock band; he had become a recognized voice in global politics.

He helped establish the Commission for Africa in 2004, which was one of his most important efforts. The Commission was an initiative aimed at tackling poverty in Africa and addressing the systemic issues that had kept the continent trapped in cycles of underdevelopment. The commission brought together political leaders, academics, and business experts to create a comprehensive plan for African development. Bob's role in the commission was central. He didn't just sit at the table, he pushed the agenda, insisted on bold action, and used his influence to ensure that the recommendations of the commission were heard at the highest levels.

The Commission for Africa's final report, released in 2005, called for significant investments in infrastructure, education, and healthcare, as well as reforms in trade and debt policies. The report also called for the cancellation of debt, greater international aid, and a concerted effort to promote good governance and combat corruption in African nations. Bob's tireless work on the Commission's behalf helped bring attention to these issues, and while not all of the recommendations were implemented immediately, the report became a critical tool in the global conversation about development in Africa.

Bob wasn't interested in vague promises or lofty speeches. He wanted concrete results. He didn't want to see Africa remain a victim of the global economic system. He wanted to see African nations given the tools they needed to succeed, tools that included access to fair trade, infrastructure, healthcare, and education. He wasn't naive about the challenges involved, but he had always been a man of action, and his work on the

Commission for Africa was just another example of his commitment to making the world a better place.

The Commission for Africa was an important moment in Bob's post-music career, but it was by no means his only involvement in political advocacy. He continued to work on a wide range of issues, including international trade reform, poverty alleviation, and human rights. His political advocacy was not just limited to Africa. He also became involved in campaigns related to global climate change, arguing that the wealthiest nations had a responsibility to address the environmental damage they had caused, especially given the disproportionate impact climate change had on the world's poorest communities.

Throughout his political advocacy, Bob Geldof remained true to the spirit that had made him famous: a relentless drive to change the world. He never saw his work as a choice; it was a duty, an obligation to use his voice, his platform, and his influence to make a tangible difference. His commitment to addressing global poverty, debt relief, and the systemic issues that underpinned these problems was unwavering. He understood that change was never easy, and he was never under any illusion that it would come without struggle. But he also knew that change was possible. His work with the Commission for Africa, his tireless advocacy for debt relief, and his influence on political leaders were just the beginning of a lifelong commitment to improving the lives of those who had been left behind by the global system.

Bob's journey beyond music had not been without its challenges. His efforts to push for change were often met with resistance, both from governments and from those who had a vested interest in maintaining the status quo. But for Bob, this resistance only fueled his determination. He didn't shy away from controversy or conflict; he faced it head-on, always keeping his eye on the bigger picture. He knew that his work was not about personal gain or fame, it was about creating a world where the most vulnerable had a fighting chance at a better life.

As the years went on, Bob continued to push for change. His political advocacy, combined with his work as a musician and humanitarian, made him one of the most recognizable figures in global activism. He had become more than just a rock star; he had become a symbol of what was possible when one person refused to accept the status quo and took action to make the world a better place. His influence extended beyond politics, and he continued to inspire countless people around the world to take action in their own communities.

Bob Geldof's story is one of transformation of a man who started out as a punk rock musician and became a global figure in the fight against poverty and injustice. His journey was not an easy one, and the road was often fraught with challenges, resistance, and criticisms. But through it all, Bob's commitment to change never wavered. He had used his fame and influence to create something extraordinary, something that transcended music and celebrity. He had shown the world that activism wasn't just about marching in the streets or holding up signs, it was about using every tool at your disposal to make a difference. And Bob Geldof had made an indelible mark on the world. His work, his advocacy, and his unwavering determination continue to inspire and challenge us all to fight for a better, fairer world.

CHAPTER 9: LIVE 8 AND THE NEXT GENERATION

The summer of 2005 marked an unforgettable moment in the history of global activism. Twenty years after the success of Live Aid, Bob Geldof, now a seasoned campaigner, returned to the stage with a renewed sense of purpose. His efforts to fight global poverty had made an impact, but the job was far from finished. The legacy of Live Aid was still very much alive, and the lessons learned over the last two decades were now fueling a new, even bolder initiative Live 8.

The idea behind Live 8 wasn't just to commemorate the 20th anniversary of Live Aid; it was to continue the fight, to show the world that the issues of global poverty and injustice were not just confined to the past but were still pressing issues that demanded immediate attention. This time, the stakes were higher. Africa still faced crippling debt, trade inequalities, and humanitarian crises, and Bob knew the world needed to hear the message once more. The challenge wasn't just about raising money it was about holding the world's most powerful leaders accountable. This time, it wasn't enough for people to just donate or attend a concert. Live 8 would demand that the global elite act. The political impact was just as crucial as the musical spectacle.

Bob Geldof had spent the previous decades trying to change the conversation about poverty, and now, as he looked to commemorate two decades of activism, he understood the importance of focusing not just on charity but on justice. By this point, many had grown weary of the same old appeals. The question of what to do about poverty had become a tired one, recycled in speeches, meetings, and reports. Bob knew that to reignite the fire and push for real change, something bigger was required: a cultural shift that would unite millions of people in calling for an end to the outdated systems that perpetuated global poverty. He needed a concert that would do more than entertain; he needed an event that would mobilize the masses and put pressure on world leaders to make a difference.

The strategy for Live 8 was a simple one: use the power of music to send an undeniable message to the world's political leaders that the time for change had arrived. But this wasn't just about raising awareness, it was about action. This was to be a celebration of the progress that had been made, but also a stark reminder that the job was far from over. Bob called it "the final push." The mission was clear: pressure the leaders of the world's wealthiest nations to take concrete steps to relieve the burden of debt on Africa, to increase aid, and to address the inequities that were holding the continent back from its potential.

The Live 8 concerts were held in major cities around the world London, Paris, Berlin, Philadelphia, Rome, and others. Each city played a critical role in this international effort. Over 100 artists from a variety of genres gathered for these concerts, once again proving that music has the ability to bridge divides. For Bob, the inclusion of artists from all corners of the globe was crucial. Live 8 was not just a Western-centric event, it was a global call to action. The idea was to unify different generations and cultures under one banner of change. From classic rock legends like U2 to contemporary artists like Coldplay, the lineup was a reflection of the fact that the fight against poverty transcends genres and generations.

The concerts were a massive spectacle, with performances that would go down in history as defining moments of the 21st century. It wasn't just about the music; it was about the message that each artist brought to the stage. Bono, with his unwavering commitment to African issues, used his platform not just to entertain, but to call on the audience to take action. He was vocal in his support for the Millennium Development Goals, which aimed to halve poverty by 2015, and he challenged the audience to hold the political leaders in attendance accountable. The live broadcast reached an estimated 3 billion people worldwide, making it the largest live broadcast in history at that time. The numbers were staggering, but it wasn't just about the scale; it was about the message, one that resonated with people on every continent.

In London's Hyde Park, the focal point of Live 8, the atmosphere was electric. The crowd was a sea of faces, young and old, united by a common cause. It wasn't just a concert; it was a movement. Every performance was a statement. Pink Floyd, reunited for the first time in years, delivered a powerful performance that felt like a call to arms. Their iconic song "Breathe" resonated deeply with the message of Live 8 urging people to open their eyes, to pay attention, and to act. The event wasn't just about music or nostalgia; it was about empowering a new generation to take charge of their future.

For Bob Geldof, the pressure was immense. The weight of two decades of activism was on his shoulders, and now, Live 8 had to be the final act. The political significance of the event wasn't lost on anyone involved. Bob had always been a master of using the media to his advantage, and this time, he knew the world was watching. Leaders from across the globe were already scheduled to meet at the G8 summit in Edinburgh, Scotland, just days after Live 8. Bob was determined to make sure that the music would serve as a prelude to political action. The goal was clear: the leaders of the world's richest nations could no longer ignore the cries for help. They had to take action. The political pressure was mounting.

When the G8 summit came to a close, the results were mixed. There were some victorious commitments to increase aid to Africa and to cancel some of the continent's debt but there was also a stark reality. While the leaders had made some symbolic gestures, the progress was slow. It was clear that achieving true justice would take more than just a one-time rallying cry; it would require a sustained effort, a long-term commitment. Bob's work wasn't over, but the Live 8 concerts had done something important: they had once again put the issue of global poverty at the forefront of public discourse.

The political impact of Live 8 was not just about the outcome of the G8 summit; it was about the way the event redefined the role of celebrity activism. Artists and celebrities were no longer just performing for the sake of entertainment; they were now fully immersed in global politics. They were demanding change, using their platforms to force governments to listen. This shift was significant. It showed that the power of the entertainment industry could not be underestimated when it came to shaping the world's conscience. Live 8 wasn't just a concert, it was a blueprint for future activism.

The aftermath of Live 8 was felt far beyond the concerts themselves. Bob's vision for a world united in its fight against poverty had caught the attention of millions, and the conversation around global injustice had reached a fever pitch. Though the political results were mixed, Bob's commitment to the cause remained unwavering. He had made it clear that activism wasn't just about one concert it was about a lifelong commitment to change. For Bob, Live 8 wasn't the end, it was simply the next chapter in his ongoing fight to make the world a more just and equitable place.

As the dust settled and the media coverage waned, the question remained: what would the next generation of activists do with the momentum that had been created? Bob had shown them the power of unity, of music, and of public pressure. Now, it was up to them to continue the fight. The question of global poverty hadn't gone away, and the voices of the next generation would need to carry the torch forward. Live 8 had reignited the passion for change, but it was clear that the work was far from done. Bob Geldof had set the stage, but the future belonged to those who were willing to step up and continue the work that he had started.

CHAPTER 10: PERSONAL STRUGGLES

By the time Bob Geldof had become a global figure in the fight against poverty and injustice, his personal life had taken many turns. Success on the world stage had come at a cost, and as much as he was praised for his work, his private life was often thrown into turmoil. It's easy to think of Bob as an unstoppable force, a man driven by purpose and vision. What people often forget is that behind the headlines and public applause, he was a human being with his own struggles, heartbreaks, and challenges.

The most significant personal struggles for Bob Geldof came from his family life. It was clear to those closest to him that while Bob was constantly advocating for the world, the battles he faced within his own family were often more overwhelming. For all the acclaim he received for his tireless work with Live Aid and Band Aid, his personal world was far from perfect. Like many individuals in the public eye, Bob's relationships, particularly within his family, were shaped by the demands of his career and his intense commitment to his humanitarian efforts.

Tragedy struck Bob's life in 1993, when he suffered the unimaginable loss of his wife, Paula Yates. Paula, a well-known British television presenter, had been by Bob's side through much of his journey. They had been married in 1986 and had three daughters together: Fifi, Peaches, and Pixie. Bob and Paula's relationship had been a subject of public fascination, their personal lives often dissected by the media. Despite the pressures of fame, they appeared to have a deep connection. Paula, though, had her own battles. Struggling with addiction and personal demons, she had become more of a tabloid figure than the woman Bob had once known.

Her death, due to a heroin overdose, was a devastating blow to Bob, one that took him to a dark place in his personal life. The tragedy was compounded by the fact that their children had been left to cope with the

Bob Geldof

aftermath of Paula's passing, without the full understanding of what had really happened. Bob was left to raise his daughters alone, and this responsibility weighed heavily on him. The loss of Paula was a shock that reverberated far beyond his personal life. The media coverage of the tragedy was merciless. There were whispers, tabloid stories, and constant public scrutiny. Bob, who had spent so much of his life championing the rights of others, now found himself fighting the most painful battle of his life.

The constant media intrusion became one of the most difficult aspects of Bob's grief. He had already experienced his fair share of public scrutiny as a result of his activism, but this was different. It wasn't about ideas or causes anymore it was about his family, his personal heartbreak, and the invasive attention he received from the press. The vultures circled, and Bob found himself in a battle that felt impossible to win. Despite the media attention, Bob remained steadfast in his commitment to raising his daughters in the most loving and stable environment possible. The pain of losing Paula never truly left him, but he threw himself into his work and fatherhood, determined to make a better life for his children.

As time went on, Bob's personal life began to stabilize, but the shadow of Paula's death continued to loom over him. In the years that followed, Bob continued to battle with his own sense of loss. His world had been irrevocably changed, and while his public persona as a tireless advocate for Africa and global justice never wavered, the inner turmoil that Bob felt was impossible to ignore. He grappled with guilt, self-doubt, and the painful realization that the life he had hoped to build with Paula had been shattered forever. The pain of raising his daughters without their mother weighed heavily on him, and though Bob maintained a brave face in public, behind closed doors, the emotional toll was immense.

Public scrutiny, too, was never far from Bob's mind. For every act of kindness, for every charity he spearheaded, and for every humanitarian cause he championed, there was a critic waiting to question his motives, to undermine his efforts. As his fame grew, so did the scrutiny. Being in the public eye meant that every move he made was watched, dissected, and often misinterpreted. In the aftermath of Paula's death, Bob became the target of even more intense media scrutiny. People questioned his parenting, his grief, and his ability to raise his daughters alone. There was no escape from the spotlight, no refuge from the constant attention.

But despite the onslaught of public criticism and personal grief, Bob Geldof remained resolute. He had always been a fighter, someone who didn't let the weight of the world hold him back. His resilience was part of what had made him such a force in the fight against global poverty. He had always been someone who refused to accept defeat, who kept moving forward in the face of adversity. Now, in his personal life, that same resilience was called upon once again. Raising his daughters as a single parent wasn't easy, but Bob threw himself into the role with everything he had. He made sure they knew how much he loved them, how much he would sacrifice for their happiness and well-being.

Throughout the years, Bob often reflected on his own vulnerabilities. He knew that no matter how much he achieved in his professional life, personal happiness was something entirely different. The toll of the tragedy, the heartbreak, and the emotional weight of his responsibilities weighed heavily on him. Yet, despite all the challenges, Bob continued to push forward. It wasn't about forgetting the past, it was about continuing to live in the present and ensuring that his daughters had everything they needed to succeed and thrive in a world that was far from kind to them. Bob's focus, in the end, shifted toward making sure his family and his daughters had the stability they needed in a world that was often unstable.

His personal struggles became part of his broader narrative. The man who had taken on the world's problems and fought for a better future was now facing the toughest battle of his life: healing from personal loss, keeping his family intact, and finding peace amidst the chaos. The resilience that had made him a successful campaigner for global change became the cornerstone of his personal survival. He knew that for his daughters to have the best chance in life, he had to overcome the deepest pain he had ever experienced and continue to show up for them, even when it felt impossible.

As he worked through his grief, Bob also began to reflect more on his own role as a public figure. He wasn't just a spokesperson for African poverty, a man who had used music to change the world. He was also a father, a man dealing with his own flaws, fears, and personal challenges. He wasn't a superhero, he was a real person, deeply affected by the world around him. His humanity, in many ways, made his work even more powerful. He wasn't asking for pity or sympathy, but for understanding. The experiences that had shaped him personally had also shaped his advocacy. His struggles had made him more empathetic, more driven, and ultimately more determined to fight for a world where others wouldn't have to endure the same pain he had.

By the end of the 1990s and into the early 2000s, Bob had begun to rebuild his life. The public's attention had shifted away from his personal life, but for Bob, the healing had been slow and gradual. He kept the memories of Paula, the pain of her loss, and the lessons of that chapter close to him. He didn't hide from his grief; he carried it with him, using it as a reminder of why he was doing the work he was doing. And, through it all, Bob's resolve never wavered. He had faced unimaginable personal challenges, but he kept fighting not just for the cause, but for his family, and for a world that needed more people willing to stand up for what was right. His personal struggles had shaped him into the man he was, a man who understood that the road to change was never smooth, but always worth walking.

CHAPTER 11: THE BUSINESSMAN

Bob Geldof's life had always been driven by a restless energy, a need to make an impact that could transcend the music scene and ripple through every corner of society. After decades of activism, charity work, and global campaigns, he found himself navigating a new path, one that took him beyond the familiar world of rock and roll and into the often unfamiliar territory of business. While Bob had always been a man of action, it wasn't until his post-music career that he fully embraced the business side of his life. His ventures into media, entrepreneurship, and investment marked a natural evolution for a man who had long understood the power of influence and connections.

It wasn't that Bob had ever thought of himself as a businessman. He wasn't looking to build an empire or rake in profits; his pursuits had always been rooted in a drive to make a difference. What set him apart from many others in the celebrity world was his ability to see the bigger picture and use every opportunity to further his mission. He had recognized that to achieve the lasting, systemic change he had always fought for, he needed to find ways to work within the system to get to the heart of the business world and influence it from the inside. That was where the real power lay.

Bob's first significant foray into media came when he launched his own television production company, "Ten Alps Communications", in 1998. The company's vision was clear to create media content that had meaning and purpose, that could spark change and influence the world. Ten Alps was not just about making money from entertainment, it was about using media as a tool to reach and educate people, to shine a light on the causes that had always been close to Bob's heart. The company quickly gained recognition for its socially conscious programming and was involved in producing documentaries, television series, and films that addressed important global issues. The goal was always the same: to entertain, inform, and inspire action.

The media world proved to be a natural fit for Bob, whose outspokenness and bold ideas often made headlines. His business acumen was as sharp as his advocacy skills, and he quickly found himself in demand not just as a founder, but as a thought leader in the industry. His ability to push boundaries, challenge the status quo, and rally people around a cause was a quality that translated well into his media ventures. He was no longer just the frontman of the Boomtown Rats or the activist who organized Live Aid; now, he was shaping the media landscape in a way that aligned with his larger vision of social change.

With Ten Alps, Bob began to build a portfolio of projects that combined entertainment with impact. His company produced everything from documentaries to drama series, all with a focus on telling stories that mattered. He was particularly drawn to projects that dealt with social justice, poverty, and the environment issues that had long been his passion. The goal was always to create work that would inspire viewers, to make them think about the world in a different way, and to spark a desire to take action. Ten Alps wasn't just another media company, it was a platform for change.

It was during this period that Bob began to realize the power of the media in shaping public perception. He had spent much of his life challenging the system, demanding that people see the world differently, and now he had the opportunity to do just that on a much larger scale. As a media mogul, Bob was able to influence how the world viewed global issues, shaping the narrative around poverty, hunger, and injustice. His television company wasn't just producing content, it was creating a movement, one that could reach millions of people and change the way they thought about the world.

At the same time, Bob began to embrace entrepreneurial pursuits in other areas. His interests extended beyond media, as he explored opportunities in various sectors, including business and investment. He became involved in a range of projects, from energy companies to venture capital investments, all with the same driving force:

making the world a better place. Bob wasn't just interested in making money he was looking for opportunities to make a meaningful impact, to use his position to create long-lasting change. His business ventures were always aligned with his values, always focused on creating something that could benefit society at large.

Co-founding the private equity firm "8 Miles" in 2007 with the goal of investing in Africa was one of Bob's most notable business ventures. The firm was created with the goal of making investments that could help drive sustainable economic growth on the continent. Bob had long believed that Africa's future lay in its ability to stand on its own, to build its own industries, and to foster local entrepreneurship. "8 Miles" was his way of putting his money where his mouth was. The firm focused on investments in infrastructure, agriculture, and energy sectors that had the potential to transform Africa's economic landscape. For Bob, it was a chance to apply the lessons he had learned in his humanitarian work to the business world. He wasn't just investing for profit, he was investing for the future of the continent.

In many ways, "8 Miles" was a natural extension of Bob's long-standing commitment to Africa. It wasn't about making quick returns or getting rich, it was about creating opportunities for African businesses to thrive, for local economies to grow, and for the continent to become more self-sufficient. Bob understood that charity alone couldn't solve Africa's problems; what the continent needed was a sustainable economic foundation. Through "8 Miles", he sought to build that foundation, focusing on long-term investments that would create jobs, generate income, and help lift millions out of poverty.

Bob's involvement in "8 Miles" also marked a shift in his thinking about development. He had long been a vocal advocate for debt relief and humanitarian aid, but now, through his business ventures, he was looking at the bigger picture. His experience with Live Aid and Band Aid had shown him that short-term solutions, while necessary, weren't enough. Africa needed more than aid, it needed economic independence. "8 Miles" was his answer to that need, a way to help African nations build their own futures without relying on external assistance.

The firm's investments were wide-ranging and far-reaching. "8 Miles" supported projects in clean energy, sustainable agriculture, and infrastructure development. It wasn't just about finding quick returns, it was about making investments that would have a lasting impact. Bob knew that it would take time for these investments to pay off, but he was patient. He believed in the long game, and he was willing to invest the time and resources necessary to make a difference.

While "8 Miles" represented a shift into the world of business, Bob's commitment to philanthropy never waned. In fact, his entrepreneurial pursuits only served to strengthen his resolve to continue his humanitarian work. Through "8 Miles" and his other ventures, Bob was able to direct resources to causes that mattered to him. His work in Africa was just one example of how he was using his business savvy to create positive change. He had always been someone who saw the potential for good in everything, and now, he was using his platform to create opportunities where they were needed most.

In the years following his media and business ventures, Bob continued to push for new ways to leverage his influence. He never saw his entrepreneurial efforts as separate from his humanitarian work; they were intrinsically linked. Every business venture, every investment, every media project was a way for him to reach new audiences, to raise awareness, and to change the world. Bob wasn't just a businessman he was a social entrepreneur, using every tool at his disposal to make a meaningful difference.

As Bob looked back on his entrepreneurial journey, he understood that his business ventures were just another form of activism. He had always believed that to change the world, you had to work within the system, and that sometimes, the best way to create change was to build something from the ground up. Whether through his media company or his investments in Africa, Bob had proven that business could be a force for good, that it could be a tool for social change. He wasn't interested in profits for the sake of profits, he was interested in creating a better world, one investment, one project, and one business at a time.

Bob's ventures into business were an essential part of his legacy, as they showed that social change wasn't confined to charity or activism alone. Business, too, could play a critical role in shaping the world for the better. His work with "8 Miles" and "Ten Alps" demonstrated that the pursuit of profit didn't have to come at the expense of the greater good. In fact, the two could go hand in hand. Bob's entrepreneurial spirit had always been about more than just financial success; it had always been about using every opportunity, every resource, and every avenue at his disposal to create a better, more just world for those who needed it most.

CHAPTER 12: THE AUTHOR

Bob Geldof was never a man who sought the quiet comfort of retirement, nor was he content to rest on his laurels after the monumental success of Live Aid and his other humanitarian endeavors. Instead, he turned his focus toward another medium, one that would allow him to channel his thoughts and reflections in a way that few other outlets could. Music, activism, and business were all means to an end for Bob, but writing, for him, represented something deeply personal. Writing became his space to share his experiences, his frustrations, his triumphs, and, perhaps most importantly, to define himself in ways beyond the public persona that had been created for him. He had long been a master of words, both on stage and in the media, but now he was going to do it his way on his terms.

In 1986, Bob Geldof published his first book, "Is That It?" The title itself was provocative, direct, and had that unmistakable edge that had come to define his personality. Written in the aftermath of Live Aid's tremendous success, the book was a raw, unflinching exploration of his personal thoughts on the cultural, political, and social issues that had shaped his journey. Far from being a standard rock memoir or a simple account of his music career, "Is That It?" was something much more complex. It was, in many ways, a reflection of the turmoil he had experienced, the global struggles he had witnessed, and the ways in which those events had left an indelible mark on his psyche.

What Bob sought to achieve in the pages of "Is That It?" was not to glorify himself, nor to paint a picture of a man who had all the answers. Instead, he used the book as a way to wrestle with his own identity, as both an artist and an activist. The book was laced with his trademark bluntness, confronting hard truths and offering a perspective that was often uncomfortable to hear. His writing didn't follow the typical structure of a memoir; it wasn't a linear story of his rise to fame. Instead, it was a collection of observations, rants, and reflections that painted a portrait of a man at a crossroads in his life. It was not the easy, glossy narrative that the world expected of him; it was honest, raw, and unapologetically human.

"Is That It?"'s writing style was among its most remarkable aspects. Bob's voice came through in every page, with the same vigor and energy that he had brought to his music. His words were fast-paced, sometimes scathing, and always full of emotion. For readers who had known him only as the lead singer of the Boomtown Rats or the face of Live Aid, this new Bob was a revelation. He wasn't interested in fitting into the mold that had been created for him. His writing was a testament to the complexity of the man himself, multifaceted, uncompromising, and deeply committed to telling the truth, even when it wasn't easy to hear.

The writing style in "Is That It?" was as unfiltered as the man himself. Bob didn't sugarcoat his feelings about the world. He expressed frustration with the political establishment, anger at the media, and skepticism toward the systems that perpetuated injustice. There was no pretense in his writing. It was clear that Bob had no interest in creating a polished narrative for his readers. What he wanted was for people to understand the world through his eyes, to experience his thoughts, and to see the world in the same way he had seen it through the years. He didn't hold back. If anything, his writing was even more blunt than his public persona, with no room for the usual celebrity gloss. It was clear that he was interested in sparking conversation, in challenging the status quo, and in stirring people to think about the world differently.

The book also reflected Bob's internal struggle. It wasn't just about the global causes he had championed or the events he had experienced, it was about how he had processed those experiences. He questioned his own role in the events he had helped shape, wondering whether he had done enough or whether his efforts had been ultimately futile. His writing reflected a man grappling with the weight of his own success, the complexity of his motivations, and the understanding that the fight for change would never be simple. It was a book that wasn't afraid to acknowledge failure, uncertainty, and the questions that every person faces in the pursuit of something greater than themselves.

The public reception of "Is That It?" was, as expected, polarized. Many critics were quick to embrace the book for its honesty and its fearless approach to discussing topics that were, at the time, often avoided in celebrity memoirs. Some praised Bob for offering a much-needed critique of the systems that perpetuated inequality and for being unafraid to confront uncomfortable truths. For those who admired Bob's no-nonsense approach to activism, the book was an affirmation of everything they loved about him: he wasn't afraid to call out hypocrisy or corruption, even when it meant alienating some of his supporters.

Others, however, took issue with the book's sharp tone. Some readers, especially those who expected a more conventional story about Bob's rise to fame, were taken aback by the bluntness of his critique of the music industry, the media, and even his own role in the global charity efforts he had spearheaded. For some, "Is That

It?" felt too cynical or too jaded, with its harsh views on the political establishment and celebrity culture. But in true Bob fashion, he didn't cater to the expectations of the masses. He wasn't interested in offering a polished, feel-good narrative. What mattered to him was authenticity, even if that meant challenging his audience to think critically and face uncomfortable realities.

For Bob, writing "Is That It?" wasn't just about leaving a mark on the world of literature. It was a cathartic process, a way to express his thoughts and feelings about the events that had shaped his life. It was clear that Bob had always been someone who used every opportunity to reflect, to question, and to challenge the world around him. The book was not just an account of his life, it was a way for Bob to work through his own doubts, frustrations, and reflections. It was a necessary outlet for someone who had spent so much of his life in the public eye, constantly pushing the boundaries of activism and art.

Though "Is That It?" was well-received by some, the book's lasting impact went beyond its reception. In many ways, it set the stage for Bob's continued work as an author and public figure. His ability to bring forth the same raw, unflinching honesty in his writing as he had in his music made him an unconventional voice in the world of literature. His refusal to shy away from difficult subjects whether they were personal or political solidified his reputation as a figure who didn't just accept the world as it was but actively sought to change it.

In the years following the release of his book, Bob would go on to write more, not just about the causes he championed but about the personal journey he had been on, one marked by loss, success, failure, and perseverance. His writings would continue to reflect the complexity of his character, the highs and lows of his public life, and the deep introspection that defined his approach to the world. His words were never just for the sake of storytelling; they were a call to action, an invitation for others to see the world through his eyes and, perhaps, to join him in his quest for a better, more just world.

Bob Geldof's literary journey had only just begun with "Is That It?" He would go on to write more books, including his memoir "The Band Aid Story", and his reflections on the ongoing fight for global justice. His career as an author was not just an extension of his musical legacy, it was a continuation of his mission to challenge the status quo and push for change. His words, as much as his actions, would continue to inspire generations to come.

In the end, Bob Geldof's legacy in literature would be remembered not just for the content of his books, but for the way his writing reflected the same determination, passion, and commitment to change that had fueled his music and activism. "Is That It?" wasn't just a book it was a declaration that Bob's voice would continue to echo in the halls of activism, politics, and art for years to come. His writing would always be as unflinching as his efforts to change the world. And in that, he had truly

Bob Geldof

carved a place for himself not only in music and activism but also in the world of literature.

CHAPTER 13: THE ACTIVIST TODAY

Bob Geldof's name is often synonymous with Live Aid, Band Aid, and his tireless fight against hunger and injustice. For many, these monumental achievements have become the foundation of his legacy. However, for those who know Bob, the story is far from over. His life has always been characterized by an insatiable need to do more, to push the boundaries of what is possible, and to fight for a better world. Today, Bob continues to be an activist, using his voice, his influence, and his energy to address some of the most pressing issues facing the world. His work is as vital as ever, and the causes he champions reflect both his personal passions and his global outlook.

In recent years, Bob's efforts have focused largely on Africa, a continent he has long been passionate about. The devastation he witnessed in the 1980s during the Ethiopian famine sparked a lifetime of advocacy, and he has never wavered in his commitment to the continent. His focus has shifted over time from immediate relief to addressing the structural issues that continue to hold Africa back from its true potential. Bob understands that the challenges facing Africa are not just about food shortages or conflict, they are about systemic inequality, historical injustices, and the need for long-term, sustainable change.

Today, Bob's involvement in Africa is as hands-on as it has ever been. His work continues to revolve around tackling the continent's debt crisis, improving trade conditions, and advocating for good governance. He has spoken out time and again about the need for the West to stop seeing Africa as a place to simply send aid, but rather as a partner in global economic development. He is a vocal critic of the international financial institutions that, in his view, continue to exploit the continent's resources while leaving its people in poverty. For Bob, the fight for Africa's economic independence is not just about debt relief, it's about building an infrastructure that can support the continent's growth for generations to come.

Bob has worked tirelessly to bridge the gap between Western governments and African nations, pushing for better trade deals, fairer lending practices, and, most importantly, an end to the debt burden that has plagued many African countries for decades. His efforts have led him to engage directly with world leaders, both in government and the private sector, demanding that they address Africa's issues in a meaningful way. His position has always been clear: Africa must be treated as an equal partner in the global economy, not as a charity case. Through his public speeches and private meetings, Bob has used his platform to push for policies that support African development, and his voice remains one of the loudest on the international stage.

Apart from his emphasis on Africa, Bob has assumed a number of advisory positions that give him a more direct say in international affairs. He is a trusted voice in several organizations that work on international development, climate change, and poverty alleviation. Bob's experience and credibility have made him a sought-after advisor for both governmental and non-governmental bodies. His ability to cut through bureaucratic red tape and get straight to the heart of the issues has made him an invaluable asset to those who are committed to finding solutions to the world's most complex problems. Whether it's offering strategic guidance to international aid organizations or advising on sustainable development policies, Bob's influence is felt in many corners of the world.

Bob's campaign for environmental causes is among the most important ways he still has an influence today. The issues of climate change, environmental degradation, and the need for sustainable practices have become increasingly important to him in recent years. He sees climate change as one of the greatest threats facing the world today, and he has spoken out about the need for immediate and coordinated global action. Bob understands that the world's most vulnerable populations particularly those in the Global South will bear the brunt of climate change. As someone who has always championed the rights of the underprivileged, Bob is committed to ensuring that those who are least responsible for environmental damage are not the ones who suffer the most.

As part of his environmental advocacy, Bob has worked on initiatives that promote renewable energy, clean water access, and sustainable agriculture. He believes that these areas are not only crucial for the health and well-being of the planet, but also for the future of global development. By focusing on solutions that are both environmentally and economically sustainable, Bob has sought to ensure that the fight for a better world goes hand in hand with the fight to protect the planet. In this sense, his advocacy has come full circle just as he worked to end the suffering caused by famine in the 1980s, he is now focused on ensuring that future generations are not condemned to live with the consequences of climate inaction.

Bob Geldof

Alongside his ongoing work in Africa and his advocacy for climate action, Bob continues to use his platform to raise awareness about a range of other critical issues. His campaigns have included calls for global health reform, especially in the wake of the COVID-19 pandemic, and a renewed focus on improving access to education for marginalized communities. For Bob, these issues are all interconnected: poverty, inequality, and environmental destruction are not isolated problems; they are part of a larger system of injustice that demands comprehensive solutions. Through his advocacy, Bob is committed to ensuring that these conversations remain at the forefront of global policy discussions, and that tangible steps are taken to address the root causes of these global challenges.

Bob's role in today's political landscape is not just as an advisor or advocate; he remains an active participant in shaping policy and public opinion. His ability to mobilize public support for causes that he believes in is one of his greatest strengths. Just as he did with Live Aid, Bob continues to harness the power of public awareness to push for meaningful change. He knows that political leaders will only act when their constituencies demand it, and he has used his platform to encourage people to get involved, to make their voices heard, and to demand the changes that are necessary for a better world. Bob's work in recent years has shown that the fight for social justice and environmental sustainability is ongoing, and that it requires the continued engagement of the global public.

Bob's capacity to change with the times is one of the main factors contributing to his ongoing relevance as an activist. The issues that drove him to action in the 1980s hunger, poverty, and debt are still pressing concerns, but new challenges have emerged. Bob has been able to evolve with the times, recognizing that the world is changing and that new solutions are needed. While his early work focused on immediate humanitarian aid, his later efforts have been more focused on long-term development and structural reform. He understands that addressing the root causes of poverty and inequality requires not just charity, but a fundamental shift in the way the global economy operates.

Bob's continued advocacy is a testament to his unwavering commitment to making the world a better place. He has never been content to sit back and watch from the sidelines. His belief in the power of collective action remains as strong as ever, and his determination to fight for a world that is fairer, more just, and more sustainable has not waned. Despite the challenges, the setbacks, and the criticisms, Bob remains as passionate and driven as he was when he first started his activism decades ago.

In many ways, Bob Geldof today is a reflection of the man he has always been a tireless fighter for justice, a man who refuses to accept the status quo, and a voice for those who cannot speak for themselves. His legacy as a musician, an activist, and a businessman is secure, but his work is far from finished. The world continues to face enormous challenges, and Bob remains as committed as ever to making a difference. Through his ongoing efforts in Africa, his advocacy for climate action, and his work on a wide range of other global issues, Bob Geldof proves that activism is not just a phase, it is a lifelong commitment to change.

The world may have changed since Bob first made his name as a musician and humanitarian, but his mission has never wavered. He continues to challenge the systems of power and injustice, fighting for the causes that have defined his life. His voice remains loud, his resolve unshaken, and his vision for a better world as strong as ever. Bob Geldof's activism today is just as vital as it was when he first stepped onto the global stage, and his legacy as one of the most influential figures in modern history is still unfolding.

CHAPTER 14: THE MAN BEHIND THE ICON

Bob Geldof's public image is inextricably linked to his activism, music, and tireless campaigning for global causes. To the outside world, he is the fiery advocate who led the charge for famine relief, the mastermind behind Live Aid, and the rock star turned humanitarian whose name became synonymous with global change. His image as a champion for justice is often celebrated, with accolades and praise bestowed upon him for his dedication to using fame as a force for good. However, behind this powerful public persona lies a far more complex figure. Beyond the headlines and the music, Bob Geldof is a man who has had to navigate a deeply personal journey one fraught with challenges, introspection, and moments of doubt. The man behind the icon is not just defined by his achievements, but by the quiet moments of reflection and vulnerability that have shaped his philosophy on life, his approach to the world, and the way he has moved through it.

At the heart of Bob's personal life is a paradox. On one hand, he has spent decades in the public eye, constantly under scrutiny, with every decision and action dissected by the media. On the other hand, he has always been someone fiercely protective of his privacy, drawing a clear line between the person he is in the spotlight and the person he is behind closed doors. Bob's relationship with fame has always been complicated. It's not that he sought the attention; rather, he understood the power it gave him to effect change. He knew that to make a real difference, he would need to step into the public eye, to leverage his fame in the service of causes that mattered. Yet, in the quiet moments away from the cameras, Bob has been just like any other person grappling with personal pain, wrestling with his identity, and seeking a balance between the demands of his public life and the needs of his family and personal well-being.

Bob's personal life has often been marked by tragedy, but also by love, resilience, and a sense of responsibility toward those closest to him. His marriage to Paula Yates, although at times turbulent and filled with the complexities that come with celebrity, was one of the most significant relationships of his life. Their partnership, despite the ups and downs, resulted in three daughters Fifi, Peaches, and Pixie whom Bob has always considered his greatest accomplishment. After Paula's tragic death in 2000, Bob's life took a turn that none could have predicted. The grief from losing Paula, a woman he had loved deeply, shook him to his core. Yet, through the pain, Bob's commitment to his daughters never wavered. In the aftermath of such a devastating loss, he channeled his energy into raising his children, prioritizing their well-being and attempting to create a sense of normalcy in their lives amidst the chaos of media attention and personal heartbreak.

Though his personal life has been marked by public struggles, Bob has always remained grounded in his role as a father. His devotion to his daughters has been a central theme throughout his life. The loss of Paula, coupled with the media frenzy that surrounded her death, only deepened Bob's commitment to being present for his children, to ensuring that they grew up knowing they were loved and supported. His journey as a single father wasn't one that he had planned, but it was one that he embraced fully. Bob understood the importance of raising his daughters with love, patience, and understanding, and he made it his mission to shield them from the harsh glare of the spotlight whenever possible. His relationship with his children, particularly as they grew into adulthood, has been one of mutual respect and love, and Bob has often spoken about how proud he is of the individuals they have become.

Yet, even as a father, Bob has never fully separated himself from the public. His personal philosophies and beliefs have shaped the way he lives, not only as a man behind closed doors but as someone who has used every part of his life to fuel a larger mission. Bob's beliefs are rooted in a deep sense of justice. From a young age, he questioned authority, challenged societal norms, and sought to understand the inequalities that existed in the world. His rebellious nature, which once found expression through music, later evolved into activism.

Bob's belief in fairness, in the power of collective action, and in the importance of standing up for the voiceless drove him to engage with the political, social, and economic systems that perpetuated inequality. He became a man who not only spoke out against the world's injustices but also sought to find tangible solutions to them.

For Bob, politics and activism are not separate from personal philosophy; they are expressions of his deepest beliefs. The idea of fairness, of a world where every person has the right to be treated with dignity and respect, has always been central to his worldview. In his eyes, the fight for equality is not just about fighting for a specific group of people; it is about fighting for humanity as a whole. His philosophy isn't based on ideology but on the simple belief that people should be treated as equals, regardless of their background, race, or socio-economic status. This belief is at the core of his activism and has informed every aspect of his work, from his humanitarian efforts to his advocacy for debt relief and his calls for global climate action.

Public persona, however, is often different from private reflection. For Bob, the man who has spent decades in the public eye, the contrast between who he is in the spotlight and who he is in private has been something he has constantly navigated. The public image of Bob Geldof fiery, bold, and uncompromising is one that has been hard-won. He built his public persona not just through his musical success, but through his unwavering commitment to his causes. In the media, he is often portrayed as a larger-than-life figure, a man who stands at the forefront of the global stage, advocating for the causes that matter to him. It's an image that Bob has learned to embrace, knowing that it allows him to reach people, to challenge systems, and to mobilize support for the issues he cares about.

However, behind the curtain of that public persona lies a different Bob, one who is introspective, vulnerable, and sometimes unsure. He has never shied away from acknowledging his own flaws or weaknesses, and it is this honesty that makes him both relatable and inspiring.

Bob Geldof

He is, in many ways, a contradiction, a man of action and ambition, yet also a man who has struggled with loss, with guilt, and with the weight of responsibility. The man behind the icon is not some perfect figure; he is a real person who, like all of us, faces challenges, makes mistakes, and wrestles with his own demons.

Private reflection has always been a crucial part of Bob's life. He may have spent much of his career in the public eye, but that doesn't mean he hasn't had moments of doubt. In fact, some of his most defining moments have come when he has stepped back, taken a breath, and reflected on his journey. He has always been willing to question himself, to look inward and ask whether the work he has done has been enough, whether it has truly made a difference. It is in these moments of self-reflection that Bob's true character emerges. He is not the brash, outspoken activist that the world sees on the stage; he is a man who feels deeply, who grapples with his own humanity, and who constantly strives to live in a way that is consistent with his values.

Bob's private reflections are often about the balance between the work he has done and the life he has lived. He has spent so much of his time fighting for others, trying to right the wrongs of the world, that he has sometimes struggled to find balance in his personal life. The demands of public life have often left little room for the quiet moments of introspection that many people seek. In the quiet, away from the cameras and the adoring fans, Bob has had to ask himself some tough questions about his choices, his priorities, and the legacy he wishes to leave behind. These moments of reflection are often filled with a sense of responsibility, a desire to make sure that the work he has done is truly meaningful and that it will continue to have an impact long after he is gone.

As Bob reflects on his life, he knows that the man behind the icon is not defined by his public image alone. He is a man who has loved deeply, who has suffered great loss, and who has fought tirelessly for the causes he believes in. He is a father, a son, a friend, and a mentor, and these roles are just as important to him as the public accolades he has received. Bob has never been one to rest on his laurels, and he continues to work, to fight, and to reflect on how he can make the world a better place. Behind the icon is a man whose commitment to justice, to fairness, and to making a difference continues to drive him forward, even when the road ahead seems uncertain. It is this combination of strength and vulnerability, of public action and private reflection, that defines Bob Geldof, the man behind the icon.

CHAPTER 15: THE ENDURING LEGACY

Bob Geldof's legacy is one that transcends borders, genres, and generations. His influence stretches across music, activism, and philanthropy, shaping not only the way we view celebrity, but also the way we engage with global issues. From his early days with the Boomtown Rats to his pivotal role in Live Aid, his journey has been marked by a profound commitment to making the world a better place. As the years have passed, Bob's work has continued to inspire new generations to take action, to challenge the status quo, and to use their voices for good. The ripple effects of his efforts have been felt across the globe, and the impact he has had on music, charity, and cultural movements remains undeniable.

Music has always been the cornerstone of Bob Geldof's career, and his influence on the music industry cannot be overstated. As the frontman of the Boomtown Rats, Bob made a name for himself as both a musician and a provocateur. His boldness, his energy, and his willingness to challenge societal norms helped set the stage for a generation of musicians who would follow in his footsteps. While his musical career was marked by a string of hits like "I Don't Like Mondays", it was his ability to intertwine his art with his activism that set him apart. Bob wasn't just a musician he was a force for change, someone who understood the power of music to inspire, to unite, and to mobilize.

His success with Live Aid and Band Aid cemented his place in the annals of music history. These efforts weren't just about organizing concerts, they were about using music to change the world. Bob understood that music had the ability to capture hearts and minds in a way that few other mediums could. By bringing together some of the biggest names in music for the cause of famine relief, he showed the world that artists had the power to shift public perception and bring attention to the issues that mattered most. Through Live Aid, Bob proved that music wasn't just an entertainment commodity; it could be a transformative tool in the fight for global justice.

Beyond his own work with the Boomtown Rats, Bob's influence on the music world was felt in the way artists approached activism. Following Live Aid, more and more musicians began to use their platforms to speak out about social issues. Whether it was Bono, Sting, or other prominent artists, Bob's example inspired an entire generation to think about how they could use their fame for the greater good. He showed them that celebrity could be leveraged to raise awareness, to spark change, and to mobilize millions of people behind important causes. Bob's contribution to music was never just about the records he made, it was about the legacy of activism that he instilled in the musicians who followed him.

The charitable world owes a great debt to Bob Geldof. Before Live Aid, fundraising through music was almost unheard of on such a grand scale. Bob's vision for Band Aid, and the subsequent Live Aid concert, revolutionized how charity was approached. He made it clear that it wasn't enough to simply donate money and hope for the best. What he created was something far more lasting: a global movement. His ability to use his fame and connections to unite artists, governments, and people across the globe for the cause of famine relief changed the way the world viewed charity. Live Aid proved that charitable efforts could be both spectacular and effective, that it was possible to entertain millions and, in the process, raise millions to fight hunger, poverty, and injustice.

Through his work with Live Aid and Band Aid, Bob also made charity something that was visible, exciting, and inclusive. He didn't just ask for money, he gave people a way to actively participate, to feel as if they were part of something larger than themselves. The concerts were a moment of unity, a time when people from different countries and cultures could come together to help those in need. By bringing together so many diverse voices and musical acts, Bob made it clear that charity was not just for the elite, it was something that everyone could be part of. In doing so, he helped redefine what charity meant in the modern world, proving that it could be both impactful and inspiring.

The success of Live Aid also had a long-lasting impact on the way we think about global responsibility. For Bob, the battle didn't end with the concerts. His relentless campaigning for debt relief, trade reform, and international cooperation set the stage for ongoing discussions about Africa's development. He understood that the fight against poverty and inequality was not a one-time event, it was a long-term commitment. He became a champion for Africa, advocating for its economic independence and pushing for debt forgiveness in ways that had never been done before. His political advocacy helped shine a light on the systemic issues that caused suffering in the developing world, and his work continues to influence the way we think about global economic policies today.

The fact that Bob has motivated subsequent generations to take action is among his most enduring legacies. His work has shown that one person, no matter their

Bob Geldof

background or celebrity status, can make a difference in the world. Bob's commitment to activism has inspired countless individuals to use their own platforms, whether large or small, to create change. He has shown young people that they don't have to be wealthy or famous to have an impact, they just need to have the will to act. Through his example, Bob has proven that the power of one voice, when amplified by passion and determination, can create waves of change that ripple through society.

The cultural impact of Bob Geldof's work extends beyond his influence on the music industry and charity. He has become a symbol of what it means to stand up for what's right, to fight for those who cannot fight for themselves, and to never accept the world as it is. His efforts to tackle poverty, injustice, and inequality have made him a cultural icon, someone whose influence extends far beyond the realms of music and activism. He has shown the world that celebrity can be used for something greater than fame; it can be a tool for social justice and change.

In many ways, Bob's legacy is also tied to his resilience. Over the years, he has faced personal tragedy, public scrutiny, and the inevitable challenges that come with being a high-profile figure in the world of global activism. Yet, through it all, he has remained steadfast in his mission. The setbacks and criticisms have only fueled his determination to continue fighting for the causes that matter most. Bob's perseverance in the face of adversity is one of the qualities that has endeared him to so many people around the world. He has shown that even in the most difficult times, it's possible to rise above, to keep moving forward, and to continue making a difference.

Bob Geldof's life is a testament to the power of action, the importance of resilience, and the impact that one person can have on the world. His legacy is not defined by his fame or his wealth, but by the work he has done to make the world a better place. From his work in music to his advocacy for Africa, his commitment to charity, and his relentless push for global change, Bob has proven that it is possible to create a legacy that transcends personal achievement. His life's work continues to inspire, to challenge, and to remind us that change is possible if we have the courage to act.

As Bob reflects on his journey, it's clear that his legacy is far from over. His work continues to inspire new generations of activists, musicians, and philanthropists. The causes he championed remain at the forefront of global discussions, and his example serves as a reminder that we all have a role to play in making the world a better place. The enduring legacy of Bob Geldof is one of action, passion, and an unwavering commitment to justice. It is a legacy that will continue to shape the world for years to come, and it is a testament to the incredible power of one person's voice when it is used for good.

CONCLUSION

Bob Geldof's life journey is one that speaks to the very core of what it means to be human: the struggles, the triumphs, the moments of doubt, and the bursts of hope that define us all. His story is not just that of a musician turned philanthropist, but of a man whose passion, resilience, and refusal to accept the world as it is have left an indelible mark on both the music industry and the world stage. His unwavering belief that change is possible, if we're willing to fight for it, has transformed not only the lives of millions in Africa but also countless others who have been inspired by his commitment to justice, equality, and compassion.

Bob's evolution from a punk rock star with a rebellious spirit to a global advocate for famine relief, debt forgiveness, and social justice is a testament to the power of purpose. He didn't just use his fame to fuel his own success he used it to illuminate the suffering of those often ignored, those who had no voice. From his bold stance against poverty in Ethiopia to his tireless campaign for debt relief in Africa, Bob Geldof demonstrated that one person, driven by an unshakable resolve, could change the course of history. His vision wasn't about accolades or recognition, it was about making a real, tangible difference. And in doing so, he forever altered the way the world perceives the role of celebrity in activism.

Reflecting on Bob's journey, we find ourselves faced with some key lessons. First, we learn that action is everything. The world is full of people who recognize the problems but fail to act. Bob's story teaches us that the true difference-makers are those who act, regardless of the odds. His story is a powerful reminder that even in the face of personal adversity or public criticism, the commitment to doing what is right is worth every sacrifice. Second, we learn that one voice can be a catalyst for an entire movement. Bob Geldof's success was never in his fame as a musician, but in his ability to mobilize others, to use his platform to create change, and to ignite a global conversation about poverty, hunger, and inequality.

Bob's impact is not limited to the pages of history or the archives of music. It lives on in the countless individuals who continue to take up the mantle he set down. His legacy is one that continues to inspire new generations to act, to speak out, and to never accept the status quo. In his life, we see the potential we all have to make the world better, no matter where we start or how daunting the challenges may seem. His determination to fight for justice, not just as a celebrity but as a human being, has shown us that everyone has the capacity for greatness if they have the courage to pursue it.

As you close the pages of this biography, I hope that Bob's story will stay with you, urging you to take action in your own life. Whether it's standing up for the marginalized, speaking out against injustice, or simply striving to be a force for good in the world, Bob's journey reminds us that no effort is too small. The lessons from his life are not just about changing the world, they're about changing ourselves. Bob didn't wait for someone else to fix the world. He didn't wait for the

Bob Geldof

perfect moment. He saw a problem, and he acted. That is the spirit we should all strive to embody.

This book isn't just about the life of Bob Geldof, it's about you, the reader, and the world you can shape. It's about understanding that the power to make a difference lies within you. Every challenge you face, every obstacle you overcome, becomes part of the legacy you leave behind. Just as Bob used his platform to lift others, so too can we all use our voices, our time, and our resources to contribute to causes greater than ourselves. Every action, no matter how small it seems, contributes to the collective fight for a better world.

Bob's work is far from finished, and his advocacy continues to resonate in the world today. He's a man who never believed in resting on his laurels; he understood that the fight for justice and equality was a lifelong commitment. And so, as you walk away from Bob's story, know that his fight is your fight. It is the fight of everyone who believes in a more equitable, just world. His legacy isn't just a chapter of history, it's a movement, and the baton is being passed down to you, to future generations, to everyone willing to step up and speak out.

Thank you for taking the time to read Bob's story. I hope this book has inspired you, challenged you, and sparked something deep within you. We are all part of this shared human experience, and we all have the power to create change. The world can be shaped by our collective efforts by the decisions we make, the causes we support, and the ways we act when faced with adversity. So, as you reflect on Bob's incredible journey, remember that his example is there for all of us to follow. The same tenacity, the same drive to make the world a better place, is within you. You, too, can make a difference.

In closing, I want to wish you all the best as you embark on your own journey. May you be inspired to live your life with purpose, passion, and resilience. May you face challenges with courage and keep pushing forward, knowing that the road to creating change is never easy, but always worth it. Bob Geldof's legacy is proof of that.

His life shows us that even in the face of overwhelming odds, it's possible to make an impact. As you continue your own path, may you find the strength to stand up for what's right and work toward a better, more just world. May your journey be filled with the same determination and compassion that made Bob's legacy endure. Thank you for reading, and may you always strive to make the world a better place, just as Bob Geldof did.

Printed in Dunstable, United Kingdom